Discernment: How Do Your Emotions Affect Moral Decision-Making?

Dan Desmarques

Published by 22 Lions, 2021.

Table of Contents

Copyright Page

Discernment: How Do Your Emotions Affect Moral Decision-Making?

By Dan Desmarques

About

Publisher & Bookstore: 22Lions.com

Author: Biolinky.co/dandesmarques

Introduction

Planet Earth is going through many transitions — social, economical, and spiritual —, and a better understanding is needed of how to differentiate the paths that are being presented in order to make the rights decisions.

Discernment is the main ability that one needs when wanting to know himself better, in order to conquer higher goals in life and go through the many challenges with the conviction that he is on the right path.

Many speak of oneness and faith, but few dare to speak about discernment, because you can only discern that which you can see, and once you can see things as they are, nobody can control you.

That state requires a perception of the potentialities in you, as the more you can see, the more of the new world will be revealed to you as well.

As you ascend to a higher state of perception, you don't cease being who you are, but instead, become more practical and faster in your decisions.

Such a capacity will make you more confident and less doubtful or fearful when having to let go of something or someone. And a bright future awaits those who have the courage to accept it and are not afraid of the consequences of their decisions.

Chapter 1 - Understanding the Social Chaos

It takes a while for us to know others but also to know ourselves.

We often think that we will get to know ourselves through others, but all that this process does is convince us that we are what others see. And such a conclusion neglects the eternity of our spirit.

Truly, it is easier to know oneself than it is to know others. And yet, we can hardly know ourselves, except through others.

This said, it is not as important what we think of ourselves, as how we perceive ourselves through the eyes and discernment of others.

Nobody likes to be disrespected, humiliated, or insulted in any way, because we inherently believe in our immortality as a soul, and we need our dignity to evolve. This is what makes us a big family. We all need each other. Nobody is better than anyone else.

The prophet needs his followers to get his message delivered and absorbed by the culture of the society, and society needs its artists and scholars to help in the transition from the very high to the very low.

We call that methodology education but it is actually the art of indoctrinating in the forms and repetitions that we may never understand.

The books that we create and use to communicate those higher truths are the tools of transition, from the foolishness to the clarity of mind and actions — the efficiency that leads us, like a boat in a storm of ignorance, to where we want and need to go.

In this path that takes us through *terra incognita*, some cultures prove themselves more fertile than others, to help us grow and become more who we are destined to be. But my journeys through the world have shown me that not always are the best places to be those we could expect, for historical or geographical reasons.

The Balkan peninsula has surprised me in a very positive manner, for the politeness of its people, and the relaxing feeling one gets from the culture. And this, despite all the wars they faced throughout their history.

In recent times, after experiencing living in the city center of many famous countries, I came to the conclusion that areas that are near parks and far from the busy centers are better for my mind and emotional stability.

I may not experience so much chaos as those in the city centers, but quite a lot of this chaos is actually a void of self-centered minds that tend to replicate their own expectations.

We often attract more easily what others expect for themselves when among many people. In this sense, highly populated city centers, are great for promiscuity, mistakes, insults, crime, and anger. You know, everything people absorb from movies, because they rarely think for themselves, and care more about entertainment, even when it comes in the form of brainwashing propaganda.

This is why you can't really know yourself in the middle of social chaos. If anything, it is better to allow oneself to surrender to nature because nature brings us closer to our spiritual self.

When I sit in front of a lake, relaxing, I get more results than I would in a whole day looking at people passing by, or even if I talked to most of them. I also feel happier.

Talking to most people these days depresses me so much, that I often lose the motivation and capacity to write.

You see, whatsoever you want to do, requires certain mental patterns, and those mental patterns are the software you use to create the program — the active work.

Work shapes our thinking but so do our interactions. If what you do creates a wider gap with society, pushing yourself into society will cause patterns — needed to do something that society isn't interested in doing, such as creating something useful and outside the norms —, to break apart in you.

DISCERNMENT: HOW DO YOUR EMOTIONS AFFECT MORAL DECISION-MAKING?

Many may disagree and say that it depends on whom we meet and interact with. But to them, I say: Good luck in finding someone that doesn't match the rest of society in the middle of society.

Chapter 2 - The Problem with Social Expectations

The greatest challenge of the artist is to bridge that which is unrelated to society with society itself, and then bring the very high to the very low, by merging two opposing realities. This is why artists are so important in the world.

A writer that can't do this is a very bad writer.

I have met many of such writers. They think they are very important because nobody understands them and nobody is interested in what they write. They think that makes them superior.

What should I then conclude of them, when they meet me? I wrote more than four hundred books, and many of them wrote one, but assume they are more important than me.

What should we call that? Delusion? Insanity? Intellectual stupidity?

You see, a person may have a Ph.D. or Masters Degree, or some other fancy academic title, and be very proficient in debating art and literature, but that doesn't make him or her a genius or an interesting person.

I remember when once I attended a meeting for writers, and they asked me:

— "What are you writing lately?"

It is like asking a lion: "What are you hunting lately?"

Could someone be more of a writer than I am? Would I be more visible to them if I wrote a thousand books? Probably, I would be more transparent than I was that day.

Most people are blind, and they think that being experts in the darkness, makes them enlightened.

The ignorant one in the dark is as ignorant as the intellectual sharing the same space. Both are in the dark.

Isn't the schizophrenic that can't read, as mentally ill as the one who was once a professor? Aren't they both equally sick? So why do we think that the intellectual ignorant is better than the non-intellectual ignorant? Aren't they both ignorant?

Most people can't see the difference because they are focused on appearances, but they see only what they think they know and they know very little to nothing.

I could have taught a lot to those writers but because they could not see anything, they could not hear either. They lost a great opportunity to learn how to write better and faster.

Instead, they focused on non-sense, and then proceeded to tell me about the exercises they do in the group to write better.

I never talked to any of them again, and never again attended those meetings.

That's what happens when you disrespect the opportunities life gives you. The opportunities leave you to join someone else that deserves them.

When I talk about opportunities, as you can see here, I am referring to everything you attract — in the form of people, ideas, knowledge, money, love, and anything else you can think or imagine.

God loves those who are mindful of him;

Love comes to those who respect it;

Money is attracted by those who want it;

Knowledge is abundant in the mind of the ones who want to learn.

But what do most people do?

They force their religious ideas on God and expect Him to fulfill them;

They put love before their selfish needs;

They ignore money;

They read with the expectation that the book will show what they believe, and reject the author when he proves them wrong.

What is the result of all that?

People love their religion but can't understand why God ignores their prayers;

They behave in their marriage as if their house is a battlefield and say the opposite gender is the enemy;

They complain they work a lot but can't get out of scarcity;

They read plenty but change nothing in their life, and say that their favorite authors are the ones who confirm that what they think is true.

Imagine if, instead of prolific writer arriving at a meeting with unsuccessful writers, you had God in human form coming to a religious congregation, willing to fulfill the desires of everyone and answer any of their questions. Do you think they would listen?

They wouldn't, even if he could levitate. They would say it's a demon.

That's what happens to me when I speak too much. I'm either labeled psychotic or demonically possessed.

Chapter 3 - How Stereotypes Create Fools

Many of our best opportunities in life come unexpectedly but that doesn't make them less important than the ones we work hard to find.

Among such opportunities, the most interesting are related to those who find my books by chance, read them, learn a lot, but then search for me, and assume that I am a being of a low vibration.

They actually think, after learning from me, that I am inferior to them.

If the person who elevates them with a book is inferior to them, what does that say about their state of mind?

Would you say that the mechanic that fixes your car is less qualified than you? And if yes, why don't you fix it yourself?

Would you say that the expert that fixes your computer knows less than you about computers? If the answer is yes, why do you ask him to fix it?

Quite a lot of people, read my books, learn a lot from my writing, and then tell me:

— "I don't think you apply what you write."

— "I don't think you are spiritually evolved."

— "I don't think you can write those books."

That's called stereotypes. They want their idea of the world to match reality, and like a little child, get upset and frustrated when it doesn't.

It is like the Christians who want their Jesus to be blond and white and get angry when someone tells them he was most likely similar to the individuals they avoid in the street.

Those same people are easily fooled by those who play their games and speak gently with an angelical appearance and dressing some white robes.

That situation isn't very different from the one children experience when one of their uncles dresses as Santa Claus.

The modern gurus are like Santa Claus for adults. All they need to do is play a role and eventually you have a crowd of lunatics sitting on the floor and singing "I am sheep! I am a happy sheep! I follow my shepherd!"

I have no sympathy for people who want to judge me. They think I must conform to their fantasies and get very angry because I don't. They think the author of more than 400 books is wrong. Not them!

Most of them know nothing about vibration or spirituality, but promptly tell me:

— "Oh, I think your vibration is very low".

They also think I talk to them because I care about them. I don't! I simply want to know how deep is their own stupidity.

There's truly a lot to learn from the stupid, not exactly in what regards their thinking, but rather the source of their insanity.

I remember once I was in a bus, traveling between cities, and talking to my girlfriend when an old man interrupted our conversation:

— "Excuse me! Which language are you speaking?"

I looked at him, and he had the face of someone who was very angry with my presence.

— "Why do you want to know?", I asked.

He then proceeded to insult.

— "Because it doesn't sound like English."

I controlled my anger and decided to start a conversation with this fool.

He proceeded to tell me about how his mother, who was British, taught him how to speak, even if he was raised in a foreign country.

DISCERNMENT: HOW DO YOUR EMOTIONS AFFECT MORAL DECISION-MAKING?

I found that interesting, an old man, most likely in his 80s, still attached to the indoctrination of his own mother. An adult, that never really learned to think for himself but believes the accent of a language defines the value of a person.

He proceeded with the conversation, by showing me the books he wrote. Two low-quality fiction stories nobody wants to read.

Then, he told me he was a doctor, and that he spent most of his life working in medicine and writing in his spare time.

Two books were all he had. Two books nobody reads.

I forgot to ask him how many people he murdered as a doctor. I'm sure it was in the hundreds.

When the bus arrived, he wished me a pleasant stay, and my girlfriend asked me:

— "Why didn't you tell him you are a writer?"

— "I don't like him!", I answered her.

I spent the trip understanding what makes that man so stupid. And I found the reason: A low self-esteem in a worthless human being, that spent his whole life living under the wishes of his mother, and can't even make people read his stories. A very angry and frustrated being, that most likely murdered many people in his profession.

He spits on the chance to talk to me before even introducing himself. That's the most stupid thing you can do to yourself. That was a very miserable and dumb fool.

I taught him nothing, and he will never know who I am or what he missed.

Chapter 4 - When People Rationalize Their Insanity

Most people believe old dead authors are better than alive and new ones. The entire world is immersed in the old, the graveyard of information, rather than the new and fruitful insights.

One day I will be among those old authors, and people will be reading a lot about me, and some new authors, better than me, will be ignored for the same reasons I am now. Does this make any sense?

You tell me! People read books written 50 or 100 years ago, or even 2 thousand years ago, and then wonder why their life is such a drama.

Don't you think the world has evolved quite fast in the past years?

Most people are sleeping through life. They can't see what is happening around them. They see only the results of those changes. And then they try to adapt, in a very unskillful manner.

They would change a lot faster and more effectively if they were reading the books of those who understand their world. Instead, they read books about a world that doesn't exist anymore.

I don't care how good Carl Jung was! Don't you think psychology has evolved quite a lot since then? How many new experiments do you think psychologists of the entire planet did in the past decades? Do you think that if Jung had to write again, he would write the same things?

What if Jesus returned to Earth, do you think he would speak in the same way, with parables and fairytales?

I don't even think people would listen to Jesus if he did miracles with bread and fish. Maybe with chocolate cake, french fries, and coffee, he would get a more enthusiastic crowd.

A Jesus performing miracles at McDonald's would certainly be more welcome than one that makes fish multiply. Moreover unless Jesus could make fish appear in the starving locations of Africa, where there is no drinking water, I doubt anyone would take him seriously.

I have to look at people who put my books before others, written by less wise or updated authors, as what they are — fools.

Another thing I find interesting about these fools is when they read books written by other authors of my time, and then ask me what I think about them. Why should I judge another author, if the person is reading his books and not mine?

Imagine you have a bakery and a person goes to buy bread every day from someone else. Then comes to you and ask: What do you think about the other bread?

The vast mass of society is so very stupid, I often don't know how to answer them. I am even afraid to tell them I am an author because it is usually followed by a lot of stupidity and insults on their part.

However, the most stupid insults and questions, always come from the individuals who think they know more than others. That's the case of a young freemason, who asked me:

— "From which religion you take information to write your books?"

Rosicrucians, Christians and Scientologists have asked me the same. Such people think I must have a religion because they consider themselves above everyone else.

There should be a word to describe them. Something like, "The Super Arrogant".

They think they are closer to God and the truth. I find that very amusing, taking into account everything I know. Because I can see exactly where they are in that scale of theirs, and how they think they are, when considering themselves in front of their own knowledge.

DISCERNMENT: HOW DO YOUR EMOTIONS AFFECT MORAL DECISION-MAKING?

You know, it's like when fat people look in the mirror and think they are not fat enough. Or when ugly women think they are very beautiful, because they can have sex with many men.

It's very amusing to look at those people from an outer perspective that reveals a lot more than what they can see.

Have you ever talked to someone that is so mentally ill, that she keeps talking about someone else that doesn't exist? That's the true state of those people!

Society doesn't look at them as mentally ill, either because they look normal or because they make money out of their insanity.

Indeed, it is very difficult, for example, to classify someone as mentally ill, when she becomes a billionaire by showing her naked body in front of a camera, or talking alone during the entire day to people she never met and most likely never will.

Psychiatrists assume they are not mentally ill because there are real people watching them and sending them money. But from the perspective of the one talking to the camera or showing the body to the camera, there is no difference between her state of mind and that of a woman suffering from hallucinations.

It's funny how society always rationalizes what it wants to accept, and also rationalizes what it wants to reject. Quite often, this is what makes people say that truth is relative.

Yes, the truth that you trust is relative to the rationalizations you make. But the truth in itself is never relative. Mentally ill are as the mentally ill behave!

Chapter 5 - Dealing with the Incongruences of Society

When your vibration is too high for the planet, it becomes extremely hard to communicate with others.

Everyone thinks, speaks, and acts according to their vibrational patterns, and their vibrational patterns are fundamentally of three types:

- Artistic or Creative — Related to individuals who like to think globally, associate with others, and learn from others;

- Socio-conventional — Associated with those who do what seems right, not to be out of the norm or perceived as strange and different. Usually, these are the ones who consider themselves special for watching the movies Hollywood offers;

- Psychotic — These ones are divided between the masters of social interactions and manipulation, and the ones who avoid speaking because they don't want others to know how insane they are. It is a group that tends to grow in society and fast, because more and more people seem to be afraid of other humans as if it was a strange species for them.

Essentially, we are dealing most of the time with people of the last two groups — you know, people that seem to be talking but are not really talking. They need to think a hundred times before answering you.

Every time you say something, do something or ask something, their brain is like a terminator, picking up all the possible answers. They then choose one, never knowing which one is the best. The option chosen is often the most abstract.

They always think that they are in control of their situations, but their answers are actually very predictable, as they always choose the most abstract answer they can think of.

At some point, you will feel like you are surrounded by aliens from another planet, as they all seem to have pre-programmed answers for every comment and question.

Do something unexpected and they get scared and find excuses to leave — something like looking into their eyes when they are speaking.

Quite a lot of people are scared of that because now they have to deal with two things at the same time — their internal conversations and your observations of their neurotic and antisocial expressions.

Eye gazing someone while they think, forces them to focus on you rather than their inner dialogue, and this makes them nervous.

Do you really have an option here? It may seem so if you want to become like them. In truth, if you are a creative person, your best option is to spend your time with animals in the forest.

The more you move to the urban centers, the more likely you are to be dealing with antisocial and neurotic creatures, that have long forgotten the meaning of being human. Their *modus operandi* is like an automaton, they act and speak based on preprogrammed principles — the ones they know within the social system.

Now, when you see these things, you are exteriorizing yourself, and noticing all these crazy actions in society. You not only gain more mental space but also time. Then you turn more impatient in dealing with others. Because the person that lives in her head, doesn't realize it, but ends up acting slower.

If you are focusing on what happens outside of you, your speed increases. You think and speak faster.

These things can be measured and analyzed. It is not a mere personal perspective or opinion.

The majority of the people, immersed in this collective neurosis, have a lot to say and hold on to conclusions that have nothing to do with reality, but everything to do with their inner worlds.

DISCERNMENT: HOW DO YOUR EMOTIONS AFFECT MORAL DECISION-MAKING?

Many religions are actually made cohesive based on these habits. The group agrees on a certain idea and the members are able to proceed with their lives in accordance with that rooted pattern. Everything else will flourish from it, namely, the rationalizations as to why someone opposes them.

That's what happens to me when I encounter the moronic members of the Jehovah's Witnesses. There's a lot of stupidity among Scientologists too. But the Jehovah Witnesses are the cherry on top of any nuts' cake. When you disagree with them, they immediately assume you are influenced by Satan.

It's an easy way to discredit anyone who shows you how insane you have turned to be. But more incredible this is when I am basically just asking them questions about their own Bible that they can't handle.

It so seems that their weekly meetings are not enough to protect them against reasonable questions based on their own bible.

Do they even read? Or do they imagine themselves reading?

Scientology is another special nut case. When a Scientologist violates their own laws and you report her, they will pretend that never happened. They will simply make nothing out of you.

This is something they learned from the founder, that the best way to eliminate a problem is to simply ignore it, make nothing out of it. So what the Scientologists actually do, is use their own teachings against themselves. Is that stupid or what? But stupid is as stupid does.

Imagine this if you can: You report a Scientologist to the headquarters of whatever continent you choose, and you may even contact the exact person that will take care of this case, and they promise you they will.

You then send them the report, with a screenshot of what such person has said, and other necessary proves. They put everything inside a folder named "suppressive person", and that folder is in actuality against you for reporting such individual. Then, they make you disappear in their mind.

Crime? Which crime? Violation of Scientology's laws? Where? By whom? That's how Scientologists deal with their own problems.

I have found that every religion has its own psychotic way of dealing with problems. Not so different from what you would find anywhere else in society. So why do people form social groups — religious, political, or simply at their local bar? Because they want to pretend to be normal.

They don't really want to be normal. But don't tell them that, because they may act crazy when the mask falls off their face.

If you think the majority of the population on Earth is normal, there is something wrong with you, and you should have your brain analyzed by a professional.

Chapter 6 - Evil Always Argues with Hypocrisy

Very few people will have any interest whatsoever in knowing and practicing the truth. Most rather have the truth suppressed and hidden. And many of them are anxious for occupying positions of authority in society.

I constantly hear people telling me that they want to help the world. The problem is that many such people need more help than the world itself.

You see them organizing seminars for groups, with their fancy flyers and projectors, and kind words, and then you realize it's all a big show. And the crowd eats it whole and even licks their fingers.

The majority of the world is so dumb, weak, and blind to the obvious, that all you need is to fit their preconceived assumptions of what the truth is, to make them believe any nonsense that acts against their best interests. They won't even question you about it.

I have noticed that women in particular, have a higher capacity to fool other women, and quite well. They just need some pink boards and some childish exercises about emotions and the group will take anything else that comes next.

It is incredible to see that most people just don't think. They act completely based on their feelings. Many even tell me:

— "I don't need to know. I feel!"

Here you have the source of ignorance — The idea that feelings are truths. That's a great way to not live.

I'm sure drug addicts agree that feelings trump logic.

When these feelings become part of the habits of the many, we call that having a culture.

No matter how dumb a culture is, everyone is proud of theirs. But this idea of being proud of one's nation and flag, makes as much sense as being proud to be white or black or eating noodles, rice, and chocolate cake.

How does it sound to you if I say that I am proud of eating ice cream? What if I come to a group of people and say, "Hi, I'm Dan, and I like ice cream". Does this sound normal to you?

This is what people do when they say where they are from with pride.

There is more merit in having the money and health to buy and eat ice cream, than there is in being born from another human by chance and then being proud of wherever it happened.

If you want to be proud of something more logical than that, try to, at least, know the name of the doctor that didn't screw the process of giving you birth and did a good job.

Even though nationalistic pride seems to be something innocent, and that helps in gaining more enthusiasm when watching a soccer match or the Olympic games, it does justify every single war that we, as a collective, have experienced.

On the other hand, it also justifies and allows rationalizing certain poisonous habits in large groups.

It may seem offensive, for example, to say that Lithuanians have a horrible culture, but the fact that they lead the statistics in suicides per capita proves me right.

The reason why many are killing themselves in that country, is that they are the rudest, most imbecile and antisocial group of people one can expect to encounter in his lifetime.

Most people readily agree that you can't attack a country just because its residents are xenophobic, racist, and rude, but why are these same people xenophobic, racist, and rude towards the countries that they or others attack?

DISCERNMENT: HOW DO YOUR EMOTIONS AFFECT MORAL DECISION-MAKING?

During World War 2, anything against the jews was accepted and justified. Now, the same is done against the Arabs. And yet, a white person is more welcome inside the Arabic nations than any Arab will be in a Baltic country.

There is nothing wrong with eliminating a group of xenophobic, racist, and very aggressive people from the face of the planet. Isn't that why we do wars? To eliminate evil?

Instead, we use political arguments and sanctions for some, like Poland — that refuses to follow the laws of the European Union, and allows massive protests against immigration in their streets —, and bomb other countries, often for much less than that.

Suddenly, it is ok to be evil, if you are part of a corporation called the European Union, but not ok if you are isolated.

That's hypocrisy! But hypocrisy is what most people on Earth practice well for thousands of years. Blaming the other is easier than accepting fault.

The biggest problem of the world has nothing to do with politics but hypocrisy. Hypocrisy is even worse when the people practicing it do it with pride.

As an example, the Lithuanians and the Poles send their soldiers to attack countries in the middle-east but protest in the streets against the immigration in their country of people coming from countries they helped destroy. Can you be more hypocritical than that?

The Lithuanians and the Poles have massive protests in the streets against people from other countries coming to theirs but seem to forget that very easily when on vacations in Portugal, Spain, Greece, and Italy, where the locals look exactly like the ones they hate the most — brown-skinned people.

It is very hard to be spiritual in such nations, unless you live your entire life alone in a bunker or in some cave in the middle of the forest. The constant staring down of the many people of these countries is extremely uncomfortable and disgusting.

The whole region of Poland and Lithuania has problems that surpass their history and culture. These countries should not exist.

Chapter 7 - Love Can't Be Unconditional

Many people think that love must be unconditional but unconditional love is never unconditionally applied. You can't love the very stupid, the toxic, and the violent.

How insane needs someone to be to show love to evil? That's like a bird singing a song as the snake opens the mouth to devour him. It's anti-natural and sick.

You have to be mentally ill to think that anyone in the service of God would want that from you or that it is the right thing to do. And a religion, like Christianity, is exactly that, when claiming it — a community of the very mentally ill.

No wonder most Christians are evil and a bunch of hypocrites.

At least you know what to expect from a Satanist or a Wicca. You have no idea of what to expect from a Christian because they promise to love, and when you least expect, stab you in the back.

Treason and abuse of confidence are something I have only experienced with Christians. They are mentally trained, through their sick compilation of fairytales, to be selfish, and psychologically violent, while seeing their own acts as holy and rightful.

Not long ago, many other Christians were doing the same when burning people alive at the stake for reading the wrong books.

It seems nothing has changed since. They are probably just disappointed the people they hate the most are still alive and proving them wrong.

How Christian is someone acting like a demon? And how demonic is someone showing compassion?

One of the things that Christians do the most, to prove themselves superior, is to suppress their hatred. They use the word God and Jesus but are full of hatred inside themselves.

Many New Age gurus do the same. They think demonstrations of anger are demonstrations of a low spirituality, and so do their followers. But does that mean that murdering someone with a smile makes it better? Because there are many cases of people who died during meditation exercises with their gurus.

I guess they must have accessed the highest spiritual stage.

That's what some followers of such gurus say:

— "They had left their bodies... and chosen not to come back because they were having so much fun" (New York Times, Oct. 22, 2009, Section A, Page 1).

I find it interesting how the very ignorant measure things they don't understand according to their own low level of understanding, and that they consider being the right one. I even had some individuals telling me:

— "I wish to meet you in person, to measure your vibrations and know if it's really high."

I am amazed that such people never for one moment consider looking at themselves in the mirror and ask: Whom am I to judge someone who wrote hundreds of books?

They then say I am impatient and lack spirituality, as if I had to enjoy being insulted, wrongly judged, and still smile.

I think most people would be happier to be drugged, rather than by reading what I write.

I don't write books for the very stupid, and my books are not drugs, they are not tools of personal entertainment. I don't really care about what a moron thinks of what I write.

That doesn't mean they don't have the right to an opinion. They do! But quite often, the value of their opinions is at the same level as their judgments about me.

I can listen to a good critic when such a critic is able to show me, through my work, where I have failed. And I haven't seen that so far.

DISCERNMENT: HOW DO YOUR EMOTIONS AFFECT MORAL DECISION-MAKING?

They all seem to want to stop me, by attacking me, rather than my work, because they know I speak the truth, and are terrified other people may know this truth.

Such behavior says a lot about their nature but nothing about mine.

I have to judge others by how they try to judge me. And I don't even need to put much effort to do that. I only need to let them reflect themselves on their own projections.

Chapter 8 - How Karma Forms Our Experiences

If you look at the overall demonstrations of a group of people, it is possible to make a relatively good deduction in what regards their inherent predisposition and moral values.

That doesn't eliminate the karma of every one of us in the equation. Although it is certain that everyone has a level of karma that is higher or lower in comparison with certain cultures.

It is then normal for someone with a higher or more pure karmic level to feel uncomfortable in a group of people showing heavier karma.

What we have done in previous lives can affect that relation too. And so, it is normal to expect the opposite from a culture that rejects you, when facing another culture that is historically antagonistic with the first.

In every country where I have been, it was easy for me to make friends with the Russians, and they even thought I was a Russian myself.

Countries like Poland and Lithuania hate Russians, therefore it is normal that this polarity brings me closer to one spectrum than the other. The same I could say about the Portuguese or their former colonies.

I always felt disrespected in Portugal but was always very welcome by Africans, Chinese, and South Americans.

When you understand this karmic relation between nations, and you keep traveling between the contrasts seen, it is actually very interesting to notice these tendencies, precisely because the people of the countries are completely unaware of the inner pulsations that make them react in a certain way or another.

It is as if most people were living under instinct and then rationalizing their actions and thoughts, rather than being aware of what they do. Most people do behave according to their karma because they are completely unaware of what they do. Instead, they create the conditions that justify their irrational behaviors.

This said, it is wise not to expect people to be rational or respectful, but instead to behave according to the cultural tendencies reflecting certain karma in the majority as a whole.

You don't want the karma of a country to affect your own, because you always absorb such energies in you.

Lithuania is one of the countries where people commit suicide the most, therefore I can't expect a very solid friendship with anyone who claims to love such a country. Those suicides reflect certain energy in the people, that some, of a very low vibration, feel comfortable with.

Those who have a higher vibration never feel comfortable in such environments. I distrust anyone who says she feels comfortable in dealing with dead bodies or in visiting graveyards.

We need people in all professions but you need a certain predisposition of spirit and karma to deal with certain environments.

People aren't only born in certain countries according to their karmic records but also become ready or not to leave such countries according to the same karma.

What I am saying is that, if a person is not aware of her karma, and doesn't dare to fix it, she will, most likely, make choices that make her remain within the same context where she is.

Very few people have the courage to change the country and live in a culture they know little about. Most feel more comfortable living where they were born, even if such culture is negative for their well-being and doesn't allow them to grow.

They may even think that a relationship will help them in such an environment. But they then destroy such relationships when they manifest, or cheat on their spouse. One way or another, they destroy their opportunities to change their karma, because they rationalize their opportunities and decisions in accordance to the karma they need to experience.

Now, what is more interesting, is that they can't see this. No matter how much a person tries to explain it to them, they can't see so far into the future. In fact, the heavier the karma of a person, the more difficulties she has in seeing further into the future and in being persistent toward altering it, and the more barriers she will face when trying to alter such future, in order to live in a different environment, with a higher vibration.

Quite a lot of the struggles, diseases, and social issues in general, that people face, have nothing to do with what they see or say, or even think, but something else, related to their spirit.

It is as reasonable to talk about consciousness as it is to talk about ignorance when addressing such topics.

Let's just say that, most people are more willing to be told that they need to evolve spiritually, and less likely to accept that they are suffering from ignorance. And yet, both correspond to the same state of mind.

After the coronavirus outbreak, everyone started using masks and talking about vaccination, but I never met one person, in the more than ten cities I visited during this period, that considered the fact that the virus was being transmitted through cash.

People use their masks, wash their hands all the time, and then receive the cash that has passed through thousands of hands in a single week. That's stupidity, that's lack of consciousness, and that's how people die.

There's no point in talking about diet and vaccination with someone that can't see the obvious.

In fact, people don't usually listen to what I say. They rather conclude that I am lucky. As if was lucky for not being dumb as they choose to be. Yes, I was born with the capacity to observe the obvious. That makes a lot of sense.

It actually makes me wonder how smart the majority of the population is when compared to rats.

We see rats falling into obvious traps, one by one, and then, we see society doing the same.

That restriction of movement and acceptance of poison in the form of a vaccine is the trap. All these social rats allow themselves to be exterminated.

Chapter 9 - How People Create Their Karma

It may seem taboo to say people are very stupid. Many get offended when I say it. But to think people are smart is what allows a few to control the many. For as long as people think they have the free will to self-destroy, someone else will keep on creating the traps where they fall.

Is there an alternative? From what I have been noticing in my own life, people can't change.

One of the first fights I had with my last girlfriend, was because I vacuumed the house and told her to take off her shoes when she came in. She didn't. And instead, was walking in the house in her shoes.

She was doing it on purpose because when I repeated myself, saying I had vacuumed the whole floor, she laughed.

Many modern women now do not like to take orders from men, not even about things that a small child can understand. And they then create fights like this, on purpose, because they want to have power in the house. It's ridiculous but based on common beliefs, and that is also why most can't see what they are doing to their own relationships. That is why so many grow old alone, with cats and dogs.

When people fight over the most obvious things, you can't really have much hope or even patience to tolerate them.

I tried but less than three months later, she decided to start yelling at me. This, because I told her that there was no reason for me to pay for everything all the time. I was paying for the house, food, and anything else that she needed to buy. She even asked me for trips. But was she unemployed? No!

Was she sick? No!

Was she obedient to what I said? No!

Did she follow any of my rules? No!

Did she cook or clean for me? No!

So why should I have to pay for her existence? Why would a woman think she has the right to be sponsored for existing in this world?

On top of all that, what makes a woman think that she can yell at the man that is paying for a roof over her head, food, and entertainment?

You see, the problem here is not what it seems but what it implies. I had to test her and she failed. Screaming at me was the last straw. I don't tolerate anyone yelling at me in my own home, so I told her to pack her things and leave, which she did in the same night.

Two weeks later she was fired from her job, couldn't pay the rent, couldn't find a new job, and had to move in with her grandparents.

Her grandmother raised her after her mother went to jail. Her mother tried to kill her grandfather because he raped her multiple times. Years later, her mother committed suicide, and that man never had to face any justice.

In resume, after insulting the only man that made her life better, she had to move in with the woman that accepted that her husband raped her own daughter — her mother. Now, that's karma!

This woman is not a victim of life but her own decisions. When a person disrespects, insults, and yells at a man that helps her, she will have to learn to live with the one who she should be disrespecting, insulting, and yelling at. And if she can't respect the one who pays for her existence, she will have to lose her own money too. That is exactly how karma works, and how people create it for themselves.

Chapter 10 - Karma is Not Interchangeable

Trying to forgive people and being patient with them has cost me many years of my life. If people can't change, what does a "sorry" really mean? It means erasing from your mind something you will see happening a lot more.

I have never met a promiscuous woman that regretted her past. She may say she does. But as soon as the opportunity comes, she will take it and cheat. So what's the point of staying with her for three years?

I will tell you what the purpose is. You will see a lot more than what you are prepared to see before you realize such people are determined to live miserably.

In this case, in particular, I was the only person that was next to her when she ended in hospital with a disease that nearly got her killed. I helped her find a better job, and I took her to do courses she needed to improve her mind. But what for? In the end, after three years, she did exactly what I expected her to do before I even started a relationship with her.

There was no surprise here. The surprise was on me, for expecting more.

It is easier to train a dog than to train a human being. Most people, the vast majority, are worthless. They are not likely to learn even after death. They will act surprised for being dead, explore the spiritual world for a while, experience hell, reborn, and repeat everything again.

The majority of the people on the planet have been repeating the same mistakes for a lot more time than you would imagine. Many of the behaviors come from reincarnations that extend to more than a thousand years into the past. So what can you expect from their future in one lifetime? Not much!

The amount of efforts a person has to make to change karma with a thousand years is so huge, most just don't have the psychological energy and determination to persist.

Does that mean it is not possible? No! But most won't go the whole way. By whole way I mean insisting on these efforts, not for one or two months, but the rest of their life.

The only people I met that were able to change very negative karmic cycles, persisted in their efforts until the end of their existence. They kept doing courses, reading, and learning, and made that a part of their existence.

In many other cases, helping others was how they kept themselves on the right path.

Now let's stretch this realm of possibilities to the real gurus and teachers of this world. How much effort do I need to make to be who I am?

You would assume that, because I have plenty of knowledge, I would have to make no efforts at all, and my life is easy as it is. But that's not what I experience.

Most women do not want to build a family with me, because they don't feel they can match my expectations. It may seem they do until they get to know me a little better and start feeling inferior to my capacity to perform well in so many areas.

As some of them say:

— "You can cook very well, and better than anyone I know";

— "You can do many things";

— "You don't need me for anything".

Well, I need them to respect me but when people feel inferior next to you, they can't respect you, and there's no way to change this situation. It will always collapse and end.

Being better than most people isolates you. That is why leaders and successful business owners in general, spend most of their time alone. Success isolates you. The more successful you are, the more you alienate people.

DISCERNMENT: HOW DO YOUR EMOTIONS AFFECT MORAL DECISION-MAKING?

You can be kind to them, you can help them, you can even contribute with financial support in their existence, but that doesn't change the high potential for them to betray you and abandon you.

Now, why would anyone betray someone that is helping them and loving them? It doesn't make any sense, right? It does make sense if you consider that by being a light in their life, you don't let them experience the darkness. They betray you because they want to solve their karma on their own.

Karma is not something that happens to people, but rather what they make happen to themselves. If you try to eliminate their karma, you will be actually paying bad karma with good karma, and attracting bad karma to yourself.

It is better to let them go! They will never appreciate anything otherwise! They can't see what you do! They are spiritually blind.

If you help such people, they will typically see you as naive, dumb, and a moron. That's how people of very negative energies see me when I help them. They think I am stupid for wasting my time on them. That's why soon enough, they move from admiring me to insulting me.

If I respect them, they disrespect me. Because they don't deserve any respect from anyone.

The way they act against those who can bring them out of a negative life cycle is their own karma.

Now, more interesting than this, and to confirm what I am saying, is when you see them associating with people who hate them and pretend to be their friends, but actually want to see their life in ruins. The type of friends that people with bad karma associate with are always low-quality human beings like they are.

They feel comfortable next to those individuals because they put them exactly inside the darkness they believe to deserve and keep them there, permanently. Demons always love to party with other demons.

Chapter 11 - Trusting God Above the World

I really don't like the world we live in, and everything just keeps getting worse. That is why I always tried to find friends in religious groups. But many people in such groups can be worse than the ones you find outside. They tend to be even more wicked towards me because they believe their wickedness is justified against someone who knows more than they do.

Common sense would lead one to believe that religious people would be more empathetic towards someone who is interested in the same topics, but this only happens when the person is too stupid to notice their mistakes, misunderstandings, and weaknesses.

I met some people that I really admire in some groups, but they are very rare. The majority are filled with resentment, hatred, and envy. And they're always seeking for an opportunity to be evil because they channel their hatred against outsiders in what they believe to be a spiritual war.

Religious people are the evilest of all you'll ever encounter because they consider their immoral actions to be justified by their group of belonging. They are never reprimanded for the things they do against outsiders. It is only when they commit a crime against another person in the group that they may face expulsion. Until then, everything goes, including stealing from outsiders.

It is perfectly fine for a Scientologist to manipulate and commit extortion against an outsider, as long as money is pouring in into the church. It is ok for a member of the Jehovah's Witnesses to insult you, and investigate your personal life, and use your past against you, even if their own past has a lot more to say.

Freemasons and Rosicrucians also judge a lot more than their intelligence allows them. I often wonder how many of them understand what they speak.

In most religions, it seems that they are masturbating themselves on words, and trying to get high on speeches. They understand very little of what they say or read.

It took me many years to conquer the life I have now, a life of freedom in which I can earn money doing the things I love to do, and yet, I always get people from religious groups trying to judge me as if they had the moral authority to do it. They think they do, as some readers also assume that when saying I should do X and Y and not Z. But what do they know concerning what they judge?

I find it interesting when very ignorant people, that know nothing about life, try to coach me on how to be their best guru.

The more hilarious situation came from one who read more than twenty of my books and then said I don't understand my own writing but she could explain it to me.

Seriously, people are so mentally broken and say such absurd things, it makes you wonder if some dumb alien is occupying their body and making experiments in their head while they speak.

I am very open and I know many people in all countries where I have been because I am very social, but this doesn't mean I tolerate any moron that tries to participate in my life.

Most people don't seem to understand this and think that a friendly person is like a garbage bin where they can toss anything.

Chapter 12 - Civilization is Not Civilized

The majority on Earth has not reached the state of being considered civilized. They are jealous, full of anger inside of them, and very disrespectful.

You don't really know the world in which you live until you have traveled enough, especially if your skin color is dark. That's when you realize that the Spaniards, the Poles, the Latvians, the Lithuanians, the British, the Chinese, and even the Portuguese, are some of the most racist people on Earth.

No war was useful for our moral growth as a species because it didn't eliminate the causes from the world map — ignorance, racism, and hypocrisy.

It is difficult to keep the balance on this planet because this world is full of people that should not exist, countries that should have been eliminated a long time ago, and cultures that are interesting for nothing except historical books.

When you have enough freedom to make your own decisions, you don't necessarily gain more space, but more discernment. You learn that the space you get is relative to what you can have, as a person of dark skin, as a person that has a certain appearance, or works in certain areas.

A white criminal can go almost anywhere in this world without being disrespected or searched. An honest black entrepreneur can go almost nowhere without being labeled a criminal and treated as such.

Europe, in particular, is a lot more racist than I would expect and is falling apart for a long time. The coronavirus appeared to help expose the obvious.

Until Europeans learn that the borders are not supposed to open only between countries but also inside their medieval-like minds, anywhere in this continent will always seem to be bad at some point in time.

If I have to be practical, it is worth mentioning that Croatians are probably the least xenophobic people in Europe. But this would be more obvious if we didn't fear exposing the countries that are, countries that even organize massive protests to expel foreigners, such as Poland and Lithuania.

The problem with these nations is that they don't know where you are from by looking at your face, so you are discriminated against and insulted on a daily basis based on your appearance and the color of your skin only.

Even if we could label these and many other nations as xenophobic, xenophobia always leads to racism, quite simply, because the locals can't tell where you are from by looking at your face.

As a result, I experienced racism everywhere in Europe, because I am so mixed that I don't seem to belong anywhere.

Apparently, the nationalist morons from the United States, Poland, Lithuania, Germany, and many other nations, that claim to be Catholic and against Islamic immigrants, don't know that Christ was a middle-east migrant. They also don't know that Islam follows Christ as well. And if they don't want people from the middle east in their country, they should not send their soldiers to bomb their homes either.

If you want to protest for your nation, don't put the name of Christ on it. There's nothing Christian about it.

Above that, it also pathetic for Poles and Lithuanians, nations that share common ancestors, to support Hitler's ideology, as the Nazis themselves considered them inferior people. Nazi Germany's Directive No.1306 stated: "Polishness equals sub-humanity. Poles, Jews, and gypsies are on the same inferior level."

Nazi Germany killed between 1.8 to 2.7 million ethnic Poles, and of these, 140,000 Poles were deported to Auschwitz where at least half of them perished. In other words, being a nazi or a nationalist from these nations is to represent lack of knowledge about history at the worse level possible.

They are not parading pride in their streets when protesting against immigrants. They are parading their own ignorance. But it is always amazing for me to notice that the most stupid I ever encountered always have the loudest voice.

DISCERNMENT: HOW DO YOUR EMOTIONS AFFECT MORAL DECISION-MAKING?

There is not much difference between such behaviors and a mental disease called Narcissistic Personality Disorder, in which individuals replace a sense of intellectual inferiority with manifestations of moral superiority.

That's how nationalists should be viewed — as mentally ill people. But don't understand me wrongly. There is nothing wrong with being proud of your nation, except that this pride only applies to those that actually worked hard to gain such citizenship.

The only people who have the right to be proud nationalists are the very immigrants that the nationalists want to expel.

Isn't it interesting how the truth always surpasses what the masses want to believe? Besides, let us not forget that the greatest supporters of Hitler in Europe were actually the nations that are seen now as inferior because of the color of the skin of their people, i.e., Portugal, Spain, and Italy. Each one of them had their own nationalist dictatorship at the time.

The idea that nationalism, Nazism, and Christianity are related, also demonstrates a lack of knowledge and awareness about the world in which one lives.

What do you think would happen if a black man went to Israel to say to the Jews that they are wrong and are all a bunch of hypocrites? Or that if they want to follow God, they should have compassion for the Palestinians?

The exact same thing would happen now as what occurred two thousand years ago, except, obviously, for that part of the cross and the methods of torture that the man would receive in jail.

Chapter 13 - Most People Can't Love Anyone

The worse the world gets, the more selfish and materialistic people become. Most only want to associate with someone that has something they are looking to get.

This is what happens with the women who enter my life. They look at my social media thinking that they know everything about my lifestyle, as in none of my photos I show myself working. I post mostly about my travels, so they assume my life is just fun and adventure. Then they become disappointed to always see me in front of a computer.

Everything happens on my computer: writing, publishing, music, management, entrepreneurship, emails, and various other things, so it's normal I almost look like a cyborg — always blending with technology.

That confuses women. They don't seem to understand, especially European women. They are still very far from understanding how money or work happens inside a computer. Many actually asked me:

— "How do you make money from the computer?"

It is a strange thing for their mental reality. But they care more about their own fun than from where the money comes.

On other hand, they don't know how to cook, they don't want to learn how to cook, and they really don't know how to do anything in life. But what really makes me mad is that they get angry at me when I try to teach them.

The women I met are all very stupid and I am sure they represent the total of the female population with very few exceptions because many men say the same.

They also like to eat garbage and drink a lot, mostly drinks high on sugar, and are then surprised to get fat and sick. Even when I explain that their illnesses are caused by what they eat, they don't believe, and instead, try to persuade me to eat the same things.

The Eve from the Bible tried to make Adam eat an apple, which is a very healthy fruit. These modern women want to make me eat chips, energy drinks, carbs, and other garbage that can get me very sick. They find it an amusing game, to try to persuade a man to become a worse person, rather than changing their diet to adjust to a healthier lifestyle like mine. They transform the most stupid situations into a game of power.

Who can live with such infantile and annoying creatures?

If the very few normal women are anomalies in the system, and even shamed by other females, for being normal and acting normal, what can we expect from them?

No wonder the percentage of men who are addicted to video games and alcohol, or committing suicide, is so high. Men don't really have a chance in this world. And trying to build a relationship with such women is like trying to run in the jungle while avoiding getting eaten by the lions. Some survive. But the number of efforts they need to put in is so high, that they basically need to dedicate their whole life to it.

It is very difficult to dedicate yourself to finding a good wife and building a business at the same time. Society has no chance like that. But worse, children have no chance. Many are being raised by single mothers, and growing under very bad values and belief systems. The statistic shows us that! Children raised by single mothers are more likely to turn to prostitution and criminality and end as single mothers themselves.

All the quarrels I had with women were about silly and absurd things. They don't know how to live life, and they don't want to help with anything. But they expect a man to pay for everything: rent, food, vacations, etc. And yet, they feel entitled to tell a man how he should work, and on what, or how to make his money. They even try to find out how much money I make by looking at the computer screen when I'm working.

I can understand that many of these women are victims of manipulation at a mass scale, that permeates movies, education, and magazines, but that doesn't change the fact that they are ruining themselves and society in the process. They are being used to bring society down just like the Eve of the Bible.

Another problem is that many women these days are single mothers, and few men are willing to raise the children of someone else. Single mothers put more effort to find a husband than young women without children because they know that what I am saying is true. But they should have thought about it before they had their children, and usually, they think nothing, if anything, about it.

Even though condoms were invented to prevent diseases and pregnancies, most women are having one-night stands with complete strangers without any thought in what regards protection.

They then wonder why men don't value them when they have lowered their value to below a common prostitute, and that will, at the very least, ask for money in return.

— "I'm not a prostitute, because I never asked for money", said one of my former girlfriends that had sex with dozens of strangers she met in clubs.

No, she is not a prostitute. She's worse than one. That's why men of value don't want her.

Value is not only relative to women, it is relative in men as well. A woman of value is a woman that protects her body from too many interactions with men that won't provide her a stable future. A man of value is someone that has enough to provide a woman a stable future and the emotional interest in doing that.

When women choose men without value, they are then surprised to end up alone, because they don't know anymore what value is in a man. When men choose women without value, they are surprised she leaves for someone else, even after marriage.

There are too many divorces because people are confused about what is valuable and what is not. They are thought we are all equal when we are not. But the differences aren't on the surface. The differences between us are differences of character and morals.

People were made confused by frustrated individuals that want to change society to match their very low expectations, and, in many cases, individuals that sought to manipulate humanity to keep everyone enslaved as consumers and buyers of psychotropics.

When you raise your value and the person you choose matches it, there is nothing to be confused about. Only after that you can start discussing what love is or not.

This is why I can say most people know nothing about love. And from what I have seen, they never will understand what love is. A large portion of the population on Earth will never experience love.

The more materialistic and selfish a society is, the more you can be sure that love will be the least important component of a strong and lasting relationship. People will rationalize their behaviors and jump from one experience to another, without ever thinking about what they did.

In fact, books and theories on not thinking, not changing, and not apologizing, are the most popular in such a world.

Why are these theories so popular? Because they reinforce what people want to become — brainless savage monkeys.

The problem is, the more they become like that, the more antisocial and selfish they are, the less useful they are to society, and the less reliable they are to build a family.

Chapter 14 - The Alchemical Elements in a Culture

People create and destroy cultures through what they value or not. You only need to look at a decadent culture to see it.

Lithuania, which is the worse culture I have ever encountered, has a pagan past, with macabre rituals and social discrimination. Promiscuity is also deeply rooted in this culture. And when a group of people normalizes certain behaviors, the consequences are manifested in its cultural structure and values.

We could then analyze what I said in a scientific way, but no one is interested in conducting studies that change a culture. Until someone protests and creates an internal confrontation, inside the culture and against the culture, change does not occur.

Therefore, it is not politically correct to say that war is welcome, but it is spiritually correct to say that self-destruction caused through war and diseases is forced upon a society for transformations to occur.

We can compare this story with that of Portugal. The last person to be burned alive was a priest. His crime? He claimed that the 1755 earthquake was a divine punishment.

I believe he was right because that date marked the decline of the Portuguese Empire, which never remained stable again. In fact, Portugal has never had a similar earthquake ever since.

As much as we can talk about luck or coincidences, sometimes everything is just too obvious to be argued.

It is wrong to assume that a culture is relative to a nation's location. The fact that Portugal and Spain are immersed in a peninsula changes nothing about their cultures, as much as British people are not cold because of their weather, but because of their history.

The alchemical elements — water, earth, wind, wood, and gold —, can determine the future of a culture, but only to the extent that the population is integrated into those elements.

Africa needs its gold as much as the North of Europe needs its wind, the South needs the water, and the center of the planet needs earth.

When people connect to the element near them, their nature changes, and they then become in harmony with the planet. This harmony leads to prosperity.

We see this in the United States, which element is Earth, and Finland, which main element is Air.

The United States became a wealthy nation by investing in technology and land. Finland became wealthy by investing in education and learning.

What is the source of wealth in Portugal, Greece, and Spain then? Their emotions!

It may sound ridiculous to think emotions can lead to wealth for many in this time and age, but only if you don't know how each element leads to prosperity.

- Water balances emotions — creativity, art, and music;

- Wood balances with actions — physical work and manpower;

- Earth balances with what the earth gives — plants and vegetables, technology, and farming in general;

- Air cannot be balanced with the location but its people — It is knowledge, education, and learning in general.

- Fire is the element of power. Populations that don't invest in their influence in the world, but have active volcanos, tend to be poor. To prove this is Hawaii and Iceland. Two rich areas because they have political influence in the world.

DISCERNMENT: HOW DO YOUR EMOTIONS AFFECT MORAL DECISION-MAKING?

More evidence of what I am saying is at sight. Lithuania, a country composed of large forests, bases its economy not on its vastly promiscuous women, but on the manpower that international companies use when moving there. The Lithuanians are imbeciles when trying to be arrogant, but make excellent workers when humbling themselves as slaves to corporations.

As strange as it may seem, the problem of the vast amount of suicides in Lithuania could be solved with more volunteering work. Lithuanians are proud workers. I have never seen a country where people are so proud to wear corporative magnetic stripes, as in Lithuania. These are very proud slaves. The Roman Empire and the Soviets were certainly proud to use them.

We tend to rationalize our observations but most of what we conclude about countries has more to do with personal justifications than facts. You need to look deeper if you want to understand a culture.

Everything I said in this chapter is proven true when you analyze the history of the various nations. And obviously, such theory changes for the individuals when they transfer themselves to other locations. So I would say that,...

- If you want to be a famous artist or musician, you should live near the water, preferably a small island;

- If you want to be a famous bodybuilder, you should live in the middle of a forest;

- If you are a student or researcher, being in cold areas, and high in the mountains, is good for you, i.e., Norway, Sweden, Finland, Bhutan, Tibet, and Nepal;

- If you are a business owner, you should be in areas where virgin land is abundant and fertile, i.e., The United States, Brazil, and other South American countries.

- If you want to cultivate your spiritual self, search for areas with more gold.

The Egyptian Pharaohs where always surrounded by gold, and dressed with many gold ornaments too, because they knew that their wisdom was connected to this practice.

Kings and queens kept doing the same, reason why crowns were always made of gold. The gold crown is a symbol of wisdom in a leader.

It is ignorant of people to say that spirituality is not connected to wealth, because the most valuable asset you can have, is in fact gold and not currency.

Somehow, humanity forgot that! We forgot that leadership is related to wisdom, and not brute force or tyranny, and that the purpose of wealth is spiritual rather than merely transactional.

Many behaviors of the past have indeed a deeper and scientific meaning. For example, many palaces and castles of Europe have fountains in the center because the nobility saw that as a symbol of creativity.

Several ancient fountains are embellished with statues of mermaids and other mythological creatures for this same reason. Fountains are sources of imagination and emotions. They are the perfect location for new lovers to know each other better and develop feelings for one another.

Chapter 15 - Healthy and Unhealthy Spiritual Practices

Wherever we go, the environment will have an impact on our personality and emotions.

This is also true of the place where we were born. Quite often, a change of location can lead to a vast amount of changes in our personality.

Those changes can make us bitter and angry. It is natural when we are betrayed by many people, especially people who claim to represent God or a religion, or people we love.

Most people have no value for society. Whoever says otherwise, either does not have enough life experience, or has not traveled enough, or has not lived for long enough, or simply chooses to avoid confronting the truth, because they are too spiritually weak to endure so much pain, or are crazy.

Most people in the spiritual areas are really crazy and spiritually weak.

Being spiritual doesn't mean refusing your emotions and observations. A very spiritual person facing discrimination and disrespect will probably seem like the angrier person you ever met.

If you have to endure a hostile environment, meditation, religion, and spirituality, won't be enough to allow you to evolve and prosper. You will need to do immense work in the field of mental health, without which it would be impossible to be so successful in different areas.

Only then you are able to have enough clarity of mind to think effectively and deal with your problems.

From what I perceived in the majority, few know what it means to be spiritual. But the sacred books are full of demonstrations.

God wiped out a lot of people from the earth, and led armies, Christ never feigned tranquility as portrayed by the church, and publicly exposed the world's hypocrisy — the real reason he was murdered —, and the Hindu scriptures are full of wars for the truth between different gods.

Buddha was perhaps the most patient of many who passed through this planet with the truth, but even he was betrayed many times, and in the end, poisoned by one of his followers.

The meditation exercises he taught us were not about a practice of avoiding the truth, as many assume but rather exercises that help to endure the wickedness that exists in the world.

He knew he was going to die, but accepted it because he was ready for death.

Buddha was a very knowledgeable man, a nobleman, and not just a monk. That is why we have so much to learn from him.

Meditation without knowledge has little use. We see this in the Tibetan monks who had to take up arms and shoot at the Chinese army when they were invaded.

Would you say that they are less spiritual for that? Should they stay in meditation, or protest publicly as some still do, by burning their bodies in a public square, while the Chinese army enters Tibet and massacres the population? Or do you believe that Kung Fu would be enough to beat the bullets?

I leave all this for your reflection because it is part of the so-called spiritual world in which we live.

I know about unconditional love, but I rarely mention it in my books or advise it. In fact, I do not believe in unconditional love, but I do believe in unconditional empathy and compassion.

I understand the three states — empathy, compassion, and love — very differently.

DISCERNMENT: HOW DO YOUR EMOTIONS AFFECT MORAL DECISION-MAKING?

What others think of me is of no importance, because I am not competing against anyone who thinks he or she knows best or more. I am merely being practical and teaching you how to be as well.

You don't need to be happy to be spiritual but you do need to be practical.

Many people don't know this and are easily deceived. I've seen a lot of delusional individuals manipulating large crowds, in front of me. And as if that was not enough, when I try to correct the problem, there is always a soul poisoned by diabolical spirits that interrupts me.

The coincidence is so constant and unavoidable with everything I know, that it is really impossible for me to say that these are misunderstandings.

If the spokesperson is not possessed but rather mentally ill, it is a more complex topic for us to discuss here. But there is indeed a very strong parallel between narcissism and demonic possession.

It is impossible to feel empathy, to have a high spiritual level, and to always be smiling when you see what happens in this world, and the number of people that are deceived.

I would like to be happy all the time but I do what I can with the lifestyle I have. I am receptive to everyone and very social, but as soon as someone disrespects me, I lose interest in that person. I don't have to waste my time on people who have no interest in evolving.

I also do not agree that a person has to crucify himself for others. This lie was spread by some who are interested in owning scapegoats, to hide the evil they do in the world.

In fact, Christ has repeatedly said the opposite and has shown an attitude of anger towards those who persecuted him. He wouldn't be murdered if he was so passive as Christians think he was.

I don't know where people got the idea that spiritual individuals have their heads in the clouds and spend their time giving unconditional love to the souls of the devil. This perspective is very wrong and distanced from reality. Not even the alien populations, which many believe to be well-evolved spiritually, believe this.

We can say that all alien civilizations have a religion, but one has to be sick to consider spirituality unpractical and distanced from material life.

There's not much difference between that and meditating oneself to death.

In reality, the reason that the aliens do not present themselves on earth is that they know that the human race here is very far from wanting to accept them.

Humans on this planet need first to learn to accept the differences between each other, and their own limitations before they can accept something or someone from another galaxy.

You don't need to be highly spiritual to understand this, but you do need to be practical.

Understand that nobody is an expert on anything. Some people are simply more aware than others.

This is due to past lives and the moral state of the present life.

Nonetheless, people with more consciousness should not be followed with blind faith, but rather with a personal conscience rooted in pragmatism.

The same mindset must be present when we want to help others.

My goal is to elevate those who follow me, and this is achieved when such people can see what I say with their own eyes and improve both their mental and emotional states. It is not in my interest to create fanaticism.

Absolute truths exist. Mathematics shows us that. But people can only evolve towards the truth in relation to their capacity to accept it.

DISCERNMENT: HOW DO YOUR EMOTIONS AFFECT MORAL DECISION-MAKING?

That doesn't happen easily because most people are afraid to get hurt, discredited, and even discriminated against by others.

This is why most spiritual practices tend to be cultural projections or group beliefs filled with imagination and fantasy.

Chapter 16 - How to Transmute the Energy in You

It is true that certain experiences mark us for a lifetime, but there is a way to overcome the negative within us. It comes in the form of two paths: Internal and external.

The external one involves social activism, politics, and religion. But in my case, the success I achieved has always been destroyed by the masses in their ignorance and stupidity, typical of the European culture.

This path tends to be more mental, so it is difficult to have a spiritual influence in the world when this world is so concentrated on the physical aspect of such help. It is easier to fool the world in this way, reason why politics, banking, psychiatry, and academia in general, attract so many psychopaths.

The economical collapse we witness currently at a global scale, for example, is something I expected for many years, because when the physical aspect of reality doesn't match the spiritual, society is more likely to self-destroy.

I also believe that Europe is not suffering as much as it should. But this is a topic that no one likes to hear.

In essence, I realized that the problem is more profound and cannot be changed except by widespread destruction. Therefore, the alternative, in my case, would have to be internal.

The results of this work came about through books. For nothing is completely internal or external. Everything has a reason, and everything combines for the same purpose.

God was always directing me, and showing me how far I should go. I am not alone in the spiritual work I do. And so, it is illusory to try to analyze me in this way.

Even from a religious point of view, which seems to me to be the most constant obsession that I get recently, I was part of so many different religious groups and secret societies, that it is really impossible to associate myself with a particular group.

As my clarity of mind improved, the type of work I had to do was also becoming more personal and less related to the outside world. This implied doing things other considered impossible, traveling more, and making more friends from inside the unknown masses, while leaving the people who were never able to see me as I am behind.

Most people I encounter, including the ones in religious groups, cannot understand this type of life. Even if the people they admire had the exact same type of existence as me, their brain doesn't allow them to make the comparison and accept the similarities. They ask thousands of different questions, don't understand anything I say, make up their own conclusions, and then continue happily with their life of spiritual blindness.

The observations of others must be respected, and as much as their right to live, but they rarely correspond to any truth, and their true value to humanity is none.

People can see only what their own experiences allow them and they will never see anything outside that personal spectrum, which means most people are truly only valuable as part of a group. The reason why so many fear being alone.

Loneliness forces one to question his own role in the world. Such question isn't present when your thoughts are absorbed by the beliefs of a group, a nation, or even a family.

It takes courage to disconnect from all of that, and assume an identity that is complete in itself.

I am not saying that one must be antisocial to be highly enlightened, but rather that his values should never be compromised by the values of someone else, even if that forces the individual to be alone.

DISCERNMENT: HOW DO YOUR EMOTIONS AFFECT MORAL DECISION-MAKING?

Loneliness shouldn't be a requirement to a spiritual path if most people respected each other and their differences, but the educational and political systems, with their own institutions, did a great job in making sure people believe we are all the same, and in doing that, they have created even more discrimination in the world, towards the ones that see the abuses of power, the ignorance of the masses, and the suffering that equality causes to those who are different, and in many cases better than the masses.

We can therefore say that the capacity to see, increases with the expansion of the inner world of the individual, i.e., his or her capacity to accept more.

This capacity to accept more, implies the capacity to absorb differentiations, and such discernment comes from an attitude of inclusion.

Basically, one becomes more when he is able to select more, and in that selection can include everything that has value to him or her.

That means, in actuality, accepting less. But that less is based on a refined analysis of reality, coming from a tremendous work of pressing oneself towards the beliefs of humanity and their mental constructs.

In short, you need to get angry, before you know what truly makes you happy.

What makes this attitude special, is that it has less to do with assuming, and more with experience.

Chapter 17 - How to Be Spiritual Among Others

When I arrive at a party, the first thing I notice is that everyone forms small groups where they feel comfortable, groups that those coming later to the party join.

These groups are typically formed based on a sense of belonging, personal interests and needs. And so, the most beautiful woman in the party ends up surrounded by obsessed men, the ones of dark skin end up in their own group, and while the people of whiter skin form another, and in some cases, you see people of a different appearance mixed together, because they are dressed in the same way.

The ugliest and older people are almost always found alone. Not necessarily because they have no value to offer a group, but because nobody can identify with them.

These are the ones I approach first, quite simply, because they are the easiest to talk to. And then I try to know them.

Others see it, and join the conversation. And interestingly, it is the women who join first.

In less than half an hour, I am perceived as an extrovert and the alpha male of the party, quite simply, because most women are around me, and I am genuinely interested in the conversations, that actually begun with the people who felt excluded.

This is what I mean by showing respect to everyone and having a spiritual attitude to life. You are not attracting less but much more by being like this. You are also being practical.

That doesn't mean I will be friends with all those people. It is then their turn to show respect towards me. And those that can't do that, due to jealousy, or some other issue, even if they are the large majority, I exclude from my life.

I can't force people to change and I can't accept everyone. But I can give everyone an equal opportunity to talk and show me who they are.

As you keep a greater openness towards the "why", the quantity of what you learn won't be as important as what you get from the interactions. Because it is indeed more relevant to know how people make their choices than it is to know what choices they made.

I don't really care about what an Indian man is doing in Poland, for example, but I am interested in knowing about what led him to make such mistake, and if it is indeed a mistake or I am wrong in my perceptions at the moment.

Most people don't know this about me, but the reason why I am so confident in what I say, is that I am constantly testing my beliefs. I am not a person of opinions.

I am also very practical in my life. And I believe a book that answers your questions is more important than a library that doesn't. That is why I am convinced that my books are among the best humanity has ever seen. But I don't just believe this, I allow my readers to prove me right, and they often do.

If many readers that go through thousands and thousands of books did not believe this, I would not believe it either.

I may be very critical of the world in which we live, but only because I have seen what my wisdom, which is not from this world, has done to improve the life of many people in truly many areas. When people follow me, they tend to become more independent — richer, more able to learn and understand anything, more social, more humble, and more dedicated to God.

Unfortunately, this is not what most seek. But you should always be careful of teachers, gurus and speakers in general, that turn you into a believer of an ideology that doesn't work unless it is shared by others.

Some would say that's a cult, but society itself is a cult, nations are cults, and the idea that your skin color defines you is a cult ideology too.

DISCERNMENT: HOW DO YOUR EMOTIONS AFFECT MORAL DECISION-MAKING?

If a person of white skin disrespects me because my skin color is darker than his, and thinks that I am stupid just because he is whiter, or doesn't believe I wrote more than 400 books because most writers are white-skinned, that says a lot about his or her intelligence level and says nothing about me.

Nonetheless, experiencing such behaviors does give me the right to say most white people are ignorant, and I am not less spiritual or practical for saying that. On the contrary!

Spirituality is not a blindfold that you put in front of your eyes to stop you from seeing the truth, but a radar that allows you to see the truth even during the darkest moments.

We could say that society has been manipulated to be racist, but that doesn't change your observations.

A white person that thinks he is superior in intelligence because of his skin color, is as dumb as a black person that thinks he is inferior because of his skin color. Both are playing roles in the same game of mind control.

Chapter 18 - Faith Doesn't Require Logic

When you search for the truth, you don't need to deny what you already know. That path includes it, as much as it changes you before your observations.

We can agree that 2+2 is 4 and it is not possible for us to float. We can relativize these truths. But we can only understand the relativity of the truth after knowing that same truth.

If we put everything in perspective, we will not understand anything.

I say this with experience. I was a university professor in academic writing and helped students prepare theses. I also gave classes in pedagogy to university professors. Before that, I worked as a human resources manager, psychopedagogue, and specialist in learning disabilities, and even as a business director, and DJ. I also created several companies over the years. My interests have always been very diverse, and I never thought of becoming a successful writer of books on spirituality one day. There's no logic when you look at my whole past.

I lived in more than thirty countries, and basically, my goal was to be just a normal person — have a steady job, wife, family, etc.

That doesn't mean I wasn't looking for the truth or ignoring it, or not being practical in my decisions. I was always very practical. In fact, being practical is what led me to know myself better, and stop wasting time trying to fit in into what society expected me to be.

People of logic use rationalizations to explain the things they do not understand and make wrong conclusions about life. People of faith, may not know how to explain their life, and may even rationalize their faith wrongly, when attributing their results to spirits, angels, or smaller gods, but their conclusions about life are often correct.

The firsts are contempt with their misery and the seconds are restless in their happiness.

Very few people understand this difference. A common mistake many people do, especially those that know me personally is to assume my books are only about the spirit. They are not, and offer a lot more than that.

I asked recently a friend if she ever read my books, as her life seemed like a total mess, and she said she didn't because she isn't into spiritual topics.

She then proceeded to tell me about how technical the books she reads are, as if I was inventing the information on my own books

That's a very pathetic approach to life, as spirituality is related to everything, including our mental health. Besides, her constant frustrations and failures, say a lot more about what she thinks and reads rather than what it says about me and what I write.

I didn't even tell her to read, because she already has in her mind the idea I am trying to sell her something unpractical and not truly helping.

A lot of people have this idiotic idea that I want to sell them my $3 books when I ask them to read them. That's like assuming I want to beg them money for coffee, as I spend more than that on a daily basis, or that $3 will make a big difference in my life.

It shows an extremely poor understanding of friendship, help, and even money, on their part, and it's very demoralizing to meet such individuals and keep them around us. Their conversations are just too negative, no matter how polite they are.

I exclude people from my life all the time based on the ideas they have of me, more than what they say, especially if they can't see I'm trying to help them.

Meeting someone in person and having long conversations with them changes nothing, from what I've noticed throughout my life experience. Most people are really very stupid. And that is why I spend now more time answering readers than trying to make new friends.

DISCERNMENT: HOW DO YOUR EMOTIONS AFFECT MORAL DECISION-MAKING?

My books are very critical of society, but you have to always look behind my words, to understand what I am saying from a practical perspective. The real purpose is always practical.

That doesn't mean being practical is an easy thing. It often means looking at people as they are, rather than how they present themselves, and then exclude them from your life, not because they said something wrong, but because their whole being and existence are wrong.

They are inside an emotional carousel of hell that will likely last a lifetime, and you don't need to jump on board and participate in their lunacy.

Many of them either die after a few years from some disease or commit suicide.

That is the way of the spiritual world telling them, that they have wasted time enough, and have to restart a new existence.

Chapter 19 - Learning to Accept Oneself

I struggled with what I know for most of my life. I could not understand my dreams, memories of past lives, or where my knowledge was coming from, and much less my abnormal capacities, to read vibrations and thoughts. I never wanted to accept the fate that was imposed on me at birth, especially to write books.

I say this so that you understand that I really don't try to convince anyone, of anything. Everything I say, comes from a tremendous amount of experience in many areas of life, with many cultures, and with many different types of people. In fact, for much of my life, I really thought I was going crazy, which is why I invested so much in the area of mental health.

Nothing of what I say is personal, as I certainly read more books on psychology and psychiatry than the students of these topics. I used to devour entire encyclopedias on these topics, just to understand what being a human means.

I was so lost on this planet, my parents thought I was mentally retarded.

It is hard to believe now, but I was really puzzled about the concept of being human. I could not understand why humans do the things they do, and why they are so cruel and selfish.

It was in the secret societies that I found something closer to what I was looking for, but when I realized that my presence scared them too, and they were always investigating my personal life, trying to find out if I belonged to any other group, even more secret than theirs, that I lost interest in trying to get the answers from them, and instead had to accept that I already had the answers I was looking to get for many years of my life within me.

Everything I was doing in these groups did not amount to more than confirmations of what I already knew. It was time to move on past that stage.

That doesn't mean I don't value what the Freemasons, Scientologists, or Rosicrucians read. But reading the books and belonging to the groups, are different things in my mind.

You can belong to a group and know nothing about its history or writers.

That is actually the case with many of these people. They preach more than what they know.

I didn't think much about it before, but today I really say that the truth comes through me. The rest does not matter.

I am not saying I am equivalent to Jesus because he said the same, but I do think all beings that came through the Earth with higher teachings spoke the same, and it was the interpretations of the people that made them seem so different.

I speak from personal experience, even though now I am always writing, and what I put in the books turns out to be more valuable to others than to me. I could even be accused of not applying my knowledge. I am surely guilty of that. Whoever applies what I write always gets much more out of life than me. I spend too much time writing, much more than living.

It was not different when I was a teacher. My students once told me that when I speak, they feel changes in their body and mind, as if someone was changing their entire chemistry. They said they feel completely different after being in my presence.

They then asked me if I knew I had such an impact on them.

I told them I honestly had no idea. I didn't do it on purpose, at least. But the same I could say about the strangers I encounter and that get angry for no reason. I apparently cause different physical reactions on different people, depending on their spiritual predisposition.

What is even more interesting about these experiences is that many of my students were atheists, therefore they could not believe what they were feeling. They wanted me to tell them how something I didn't do on purpose occurred.

I never really thought much about it. But had many teachers coming to see my classes, to try to get the answer. I saw them taking notes but observing nothing.

DISCERNMENT: HOW DO YOUR EMOTIONS AFFECT MORAL DECISION-MAKING?

There's not much to say about honesty, I think. But honesty in a world of fools seems to be a big mystery.

It is difficult to live on this planet when you increase your spiritual senses. You end up scaring most people.

You can create a better life, but that doesn't mean you can integrate it into the life of others and their own personal values.

Planet Earth is a great psychiatric hospital for souls that have been lost, but being banal and fitting in is the true insanity.

That doesn't mean you can't love others but it does mean you need to be careful about the people you choose to love.

Chapter 20 - How to Practice Unconditional Love

Unconditional love is not about knowing that nothing can be expected from people, and that when trusting them less, you can love them more. That for me is the opposite of unconditional love. In fact, it is more correct to label it a lack of love.

Unconditional love is when you have positive thoughts towards your enemies. But although I think this is very good, I do not believe that it comes into alignment with mental health or spiritual progress. The opposite, from a mental health perspective, of hating them, is also not correct.

The discomfort and anger we may feel are very healthy symptoms. Then, we have to work to change that energy in us.

If I am kind to a despicable person, that person does not change. In fact, she'll think I'm stupid and naive, and is going to insult me even more.

If I kick or punch that person, or hit him or her with a stick, they won't change either. They may be afraid, but that's not enough to change the innate behavior.

The solution is to evolve and lead by example. It means having people hate us and feeling jealous of our outcomes, but does produce more positive results.

This evolution also implies recognizing the reason for our feelings and learning to love those who deserve our love. You cannot love and expect nothing. This is a contradiction and leads to a lack of love. When you expect nothing, it may seem you suffer less, but do you?

You suffer less because you do not create opportunities to suffer, but this attitude also isolates you.

You can't hate anyone on a desert island. But you can hate yourself for not having anyone to love.

Most people fall into depression, not because of the ones that hurt them, but because they have nobody to love. It is easy to forgive once you have someone to love. But the one you forgive and the one you love don't have to be the same individual. Besides, when you avoid trusting others, you also do not create bridges to love.

When I speak of conditional love, I am referring to the conditions that allow us to love.

As an example, the last relationship I had ended in months, and she said before leaving:

— "You don't love me, you don't love anyone; all you want is money."

I replied:

— "The money I earn pays for the rent and food in the house where you lived because you never wanted to contribute with anything. Regarding love, I don't love you enough to allow you to destroy my life. But you couldn't have an easier one I even cook for both, because you refuse to learn from me. And I cured diseases in you that even your doctor did not know how to cure. So I did more for you than anyone else. If you can't see it, and you create conflicts all the time, I can't live with you. I cannot live with a person who screams in my own home, lies all the time, and creates disagreements over agreements already made. I can't live like that."

Is this understandable to you? I cannot lower myself to be as miserable as another person, just because she can't improve herself and love in a healthier way. Nobody should do that for anyone.

Love does have conditions. We respect the other person, we teach what we know, we share happiness, and if the other person doesn't understand what she's receiving, and is disrespectful, then we ask her to leave.

I did the same with my friends and family. I don't have to put up with insults from anyone. Nothing in this world gives a person the right to be evil to another.

Does this mean that we can't love others? No! It means only that it is easier to love a stray dog or cat, and that few human beings deserve our attention. But we cannot stop loving or trying to love others.

This is a very difficult lesson that took me many years to understand, and it started with a conversation I had with a Buddhist monk when I was only nineteen years old.

I asked him:

— "What is the purpose of love when the people we love keep disrespecting us?"

He said:

— "You are not a tree, you don't need to love those who can't receive love, because you can't grow like that. You need to grow with those who can love you back. Trying to grow among people who can't love is like being a tree in the desert without any rain."

It was a simple and practical answer that took me many years to understand, probably because I had that Christian belief that love can change people.

It was only after being betrayed and insulted by many Christians whom I considered to be good friends, that I got that Buddhist lesson right. And then, it became easier to make my decisions independently concerning my faith and also people.

Chapter 21 - Learning to Forgive and Forget

When someone who has hurt me a lot in the past, sends me a message, I reply with:

— "May God be with you!"

If she sends me more messages, I will not reply any. Praying for them is the best I can do.

I cannot share the same space or my thoughts with such people. But that is also loving them, it is empathizing with the ignorance of such individuals.

Many are lost and influenced by demonic spirits. Only God can help them.

It is difficult to help without getting emotionally involved. So I only help those who can enter my space. Although the books I write are a form of unconditional love. Anyone who reads and applies them can evolve.

Feeling pity for such people is showing compassion and a form of empathy. But know that many people in this world pass through here without ever living. We have to give our attention only to those who are awake, willing to live longer.

In order to reach that goal, what we do want is balance — an equilibrium.

It is difficult in such an unbalanced world, but this is the objective that we are really looking for.

In order to get to that goal, we need to learn to analyze opportunities and differentiate them from problems.

It is an eternal and constant work, but this is where consciousness and self-love come from.

If most of what occurs on the planet is seen as normal by the majority, you don't really have any other option (if you want to keep your sanity, and prosper with a successful life), rather than developing discernment and being very selective with your decisions.

One of the greatest barriers to discernment is culture. There is no spirituality in this world because most people are immersed in their cultural beliefs. They don't know anything but they think they know everything.

That comes from a deep understanding of patterns in one's culture that have no correlation with the truth. For example, wherever I go in Europe, people don't trust I can write books. Some even tell me:

— "I never met a writer before."

It's as if I was some mythological creature that was supposed to be already extinct. But I never had this problem in the United States. If someone in the US asks me what I do, and I say that I write books, the next question they ask is:

— "Where can I find them?"

In less than five minutes, we are talking about the content of my books.

Nowhere else in the world does this happen.

In Spain, I felt many times that I was trying to pass a lie detector in people's heads. Many questions I received, felt more like insults.

If I said to a Spanish woman that I write books, she would then ask:

— "Where do you usually write them"?

If I answer, "Mostly in coffee shops", she would then say:

— "Do you work in a coffee shop and you write books there too?"

She would try to trick me into answering what she expected to know because that's her reality. Anything else is a lie to her.

I saw these behaviors with so many Spaniards that I grew tired of the country and the tremendous stupidity of its people.

It is easy to know what Jesus and other prophets felt on Earth when people laughed at them because nothing changed, people are still very dumb.

DISCERNMENT: HOW DO YOUR EMOTIONS AFFECT MORAL DECISION-MAKING?

The practice of discernment, as I showed you with these examples, will help you in forgiving others for their ignorance and blindness, and forget them, because there is really nothing to consider when remembering such people.

Jesus said on the cross:

— "Father, forgive them, for they don't know what they are doing" (Luke 23:34).

This is the same as saying to you:

— "Forgive others, because they are too stupid to know what they do."

Stupid actions are rooted in instinct, rather than moral. They don't have enough reason in them to be considered part of logic or morality. So it's very interesting for me to hear so many people say these days:

— "I don't need to understand because I can just feel."

Quite a lot of people seem to be making decisions based on their emotions, rather than logic, much less moral.

It is as if we went from moral to reason and then "feelings". And now, most people move with the wind — their feelings.

It is very strange, and I don't know where these ideas come from, but what it shows me is that the vast majority, is completely out of control. They are too far from being able to reason properly to be considered responsible for anything.

That is a very dangerous scenario, that people keep on rationalizing with "I felt it". Because it justifies any evil action based on "feelings", not only an individual feeling but also, and more devastating, group feelings.

When a group feels the same, and ignores both reason and moral, you have in front of you a gang of criminals. When this gang is the whole of society, you have before you a deeply insane and evil society.

When feeling rules and morality is tossed out the window, any type of cruelty and injustice can be expected.

Chapter 22 - Those Who Read but Can't Understand

As the world becomes more dangerous, more people seek individuals like me for answers.

Recently, more and more readers started contacting me. And although many of them are very friendly and kind, I am also starting to receive messages that seem abnormal.

A reader recently told me that she read one of my books and loved it, and she was very surprised that someone like me could be living on this planet during this time. However, the following text messages she sent were contradictory.

She said first that I write well but I am not a spiritual person, because I am full of anger. Then she proceeded to play both ways, saying that she would like to meet me but also that she thinks I am probably a charlatan.

Such people speak from a position of spiritual misery and simultaneously spit on the hand that helps them. It is very delusional for them even to consider they can judge anyone.

In an attempt to awake her from her mental state, I told her that I don't write books to be judged. People read or don't read. It is their choice. I don't force anyone to read. I don't care what they think of me either.

She didn't seem to understand this or other messages, so after that I stopped responding to anything.

I don't think most people can relate my books to my photos or who I am. They believe the books belong to someone else. But I am exhausted with such type of ignorance, and I don't have to tolerate it either.

I don't know where people get the idea that being enlightened means carrying the burden of others. The church? And what kind of face should I have to represent my own work?

People these days have too many stereotypes and are too stupid. They want the truth and reject it at the same time. They want what I know but then disrespect me. Most people are so immersed in their own mental illnesses, that they will never be able to wake up. They have become their own trap and their worse enemy.

They think the enemy is outside, and they seek people like me to reflect on them their own problems, because they are unable to face them, but nobody will ever face their problems for them.

Whatsoever a spiritual leader can do, and very few are truly enlightened, is merely to guide a person. They can't walk the steps meant for others.

A lot of the people who want to judge me, do it with absolute certainty on their beliefs, but they don't know anything of what they say. They don't know enough to judge whomsoever. They want to judge and believe they can but they are blind.

It doesn't even make any sense to tell them what I think of other spiritual leaders or authors, because if they can't see it for themselves, they are not likely to understand my words.

Talking to readers helps me get to know them better, but while most are interesting, some seem very mentally ill.

This doesn't mean I don't respect my followers. I do respect them. Especially, because they have chosen me to know the truth. And I don't own the truth. I am, at maximum, a representative only. But I need the same level of respect in return if they expect me to help them.

A spiritual guru is not a trainer of wild animals for the circus of life. He doesn't have to deal with disrespect or waste his time talking to people who are too slow to realize the obvious. Such people should spend more time reading books and acquiring knowledge because they don't know enough to ask the right questions.

I also believe that most questions have been answered in my books. It is wise for someone who wants to be enlightened to read them all first.

DISCERNMENT: HOW DO YOUR EMOTIONS AFFECT MORAL DECISION-MAKING?

It may seem my books are not very valuable only because they are new. But if nobody knew what a Bible is, I can assure you that nobody would want it, even if you wanted to offer it to anyone.

Try to offer the Bhagavad Gita, one of the most important religious books ever written, outside India, and see how many people want it.

Most people are so stupid that they ignore the most valuable knowledge they will ever receive.

Ignorance is truly a choice.

I once found a beggar reading Lao Tzu in the streets and I sit next to him, after offering him some money. I was curious as to why he was reading such a book. He proceeded to explain to me, that this book gave him peace of mind, and it was a great way not to waste his time. He then said his situation was temporary.

You see, he already knew the answers. And he appreciated my company, saying it was more valuable for him than the money he gets from people.

A few months later, I passed on the same street, and I never saw him there again. He had the tools to perceive opportunities and handle the most devastating emotional difficulties, and he got it all from that book.

He was wiser than many people who were passing by him, because he can go through poverty, but most of those people cannot. They would not have the same attitude if they found themselves living in the streets.

Chapter 23 - How to Differentiate Opinions

For many people I met, the fact that I speak my mind and openly is seen as a weakness. They think I have a certain psychological handicap for always saying what I think, and often assume they are smarter than me because they hide their own thoughts. But writing and hiding my thoughts is a contradiction to the act of writing, and exposing my thoughts when writing but hiding my feelings is being a hypocrite.

I don't think most people can understand this. They also do not understand that I do not take my knowledge from the air, and I have a lot of experience in life, which is then transferred to my words.

Life is too short, society is too sick, and people are too rude, selfish, and ungrateful. It is too difficult to work like this, even if I have so much time on my hands. My environment always affects my work. Therefore, I cannot waste my time trying to comfort the ignorance of others.

I don't travel a lot because I need to, but because I get easily bored of any city where I stay. I feel like I am surrounded by walking dead, without any consciousness, wherever I go. And my mind is too awake to handle that. I rather keep moving.

Many people don't understand this and want me to teach them things they can't learn. I have met many individuals who want to write a book, for example, but have no idea how to do it, because they are afraid to say what they think and feel. It is like wanting to paint without ink or colors.

You have to always deal with a dichotomy in everything you do in this world, and part of it includes your own ego.

You have to allow yourself to be hated, discriminated against, and insulted before you can gain the right to know yourself better.

In fact, this seems to be the most common mistake in today's society. People want to know the purpose of their life. But is this possible without knowing yourself?

Your life is you, it is what you represent.

If you are too concerned about what others think of you, you are placing yourself on the wrong side of this dichotomy.

You can't change sides, unless you are willing to be labeled wrong, crazy, lost, paranoid, stupid, and so on.

The ego is the biggest trap in which most fall. And the problem with the many authors I met is precisely their ego. They think they are important and they are not. And they want to create books from the perspective of their own ego, which will just make them even less important.

They then rationalize their lack of importance as being an intelligence that others can't recognize. And so, they hide their ego behind a mask of arrogance and rudeness.

That is delusional, unhealthy, and dangerous, for them and for humanity. The world doesn't need more trash coming from egotistic minds.

As soon as you put the ego where it belongs, and start opening yourself more to being wrong, you actually become more creative and more interesting.

I hear people saying this to me all the time:

— "You are very interesting."

What they actually mean, is that I am more reasonable, polite, and respectful than anyone they met before. But because assuming that leads to cognitive dissonance, they categorize me as interesting.

Chapter 24 - How to Deal with Discrimination

When cognitive dissonance is too high, people have to do something else and categorize me as evil, a charlatan, a criminal, a crazy person, or something else that justifies pushing me away from their reality.

It is interesting to notice, nonetheless, that those who lie a lot, are the ones who believe I am a liar, and those who are psychotic, are the ones who think I am insane.

This behavior pattern is surely very interesting because it shows me that this cognitive dissonance occurs mostly in individuals who are living an illusion.

What to say then about those who can't believe I write books?

Usually, these are the ones who have difficulties in understanding what they read or don't read anything whatsoever.

The point I want to make here is that you should not judge yourself by what others say, but instead through what others represent.

When one day, one of my former girlfriends told me, very concerned, that her friends don't like me, I replied to her:

— "I would actually be worried if they did, as I consider them very ignorant and even mentally ill. I am satisfied in knowing that the people I respect the most, individuals of high morals and good principles, people who read a lot and enjoy learning, are happy to have me in their life."

You see, I don't care what the morons say. They are morons. It doesn't matter.

The difference between me and her is that all my friends wanted me to break up with her, and I didn't. Her friends wanted the same, and she obeyed them.

You have to differentiate the people who are worth listening to and the ones who are not. Once you understand this, you will never again feel bad for ending relationships and friendships.

I ended this relationship with the absolute certainty I would be better without that woman. And I was right. I traveled more, started making more money, and finally, found other women more deserving of my attention.

She remains where I found her: In the land of the fools.

Some people won't like you, others will hate you, but you will always overcome the majority if you can see which criticism must be considered or not.

That doesn't mean others will change how they see you, no matter how great your success and popularity are. The difference is really only within you.

I noticed that most of the time, the people who expect me to fail will disappear when they see me succeeding. They can't handle that. It reflects on them their own weaknesses.

It doesn't matter either how many efforts you make to keep those friendships. They can't feel good with themselves in your presence.

This applies also to relationships. Most women enter a relationship with a competitive mindset, thinking that a woman must be superior to her man, or that all men are stupid. And unless you match these expectations as a man, you can't really expect much but a breakup or divorce.

I don't really care about what people think of me or my books at this point, but most still think I should care, and that is also interesting. They want my attention for no other reason than a sense of entitlement.

It's not that I shouldn't care about what others think of my work, but rather that most people have nothing useful to say. They think they do. They are absolutely convinced of their importance, but they are just common fools.

It takes a lot of work to realize that most people have nothing important to say, that they think they are important but are not. You need to elevate yourself through the knowledge and experience accumulated before you can see those things.

DISCERNMENT: HOW DO YOUR EMOTIONS AFFECT MORAL DECISION-MAKING?

I know too much at this point in life, and in particular, due to the many years of experience with futurology and the mystic arts. So I already know what to expect from someone just by looking at how they think. I can even, in many cases, know what type of problems they struggle with. And so, for them to consider their own opinion important, just because the opinion belongs to them, is really pathetic.

In the tarot cards, such an individual was named the fool, and it's not a coincidence that the number of such card is zero.

A zero is someone who is, like that fool on the card, playing his music with absolute certainty of where he's going, but constantly failing in life.

At the end of this journey, when you finally know whom you should listen to, you may actually be surprised with what you get in return. I have friends that are 84 years old, that I like to talk to, saying that they learn a lot from me. But I also find many women in their 20s thinking they can tell me how to live my life. And that's the best example I can give you of evolution inside a society full of fools.

Chapter 25 - Choosing in What to Believe

What people think of me doesn't change who I am. My personality will not mold to the wishes of others. But this is a personal matter.

It doesn't mean that I expect people to accept me as I am. It means only that I am conscious of my actions and how positive or negative their impact is.

Quite often, the opinions of others depend fundamentally on what they are trying to find and not really who we are. However, when you confuse the finger pointing at the truth with the truth the finger points to, you will lose the meaning you are trying to reach.

If you need to confirm the truth with the pointing finger, you may never get anywhere.

It is a normal attitude but it never results in anything.

You can't confuse God with religion;

You can't confuse art with the artists;

You can't confuse truth with truth speakers.

And yet, how many people do exactly that?

I say these things from personal experience. An important person who speaks lies is a liar. I don't care how many followers a liar has or who they are in society. An idiot is always an idiot, no matter who he is in the eyes of others. And the truth is always the truth, no matter where it is found.

A book in the trash is still a book;

A book that nobody reads still has knowledge;

What people think or feel is of little importance to me. What I can see is the reality. If others fail to see the same, we can question the mental health of the majority, or to be more sympathetic, their level of spiritual awareness. But the two — conscience and sanity —, are associated.

The act of forgiving another being may seem like a spiritual act, but to know when and whom to forgive is an act related to sanity.

I can forgive easily but only when it is justified. I don't forgive people who waste my time.

Experience has shown me that I can predict the future of others better than they can predict for themselves. Therefore, I already know at the outset who can and cannot be forgiven. The signs are clear from the start.

Most do not deserve forgiveness in any given moment except death. Because they only change with death. That is why they reincarnate on Earth so many times.

Then, they forget everything in the process of adapting to the new life, and repeat the same idiocy of the past, as the malevolent instincts and predispositions are still present in them.

To think that when you become more conscious, you also become immune to pain, is naive.

Many people have this perspective, which is totally wrong.

In fact, when someone places me in a competition of their own, for whom is true and false, we are not going to get anywhere. And quite honestly, I have no patience for that either.

I don't always respond to all the people who come to me or to all the messages I receive. Especially, if they intend to judge me by comparing me with other speakers and authors.

In ancient times, among the tribes, friendly gestures, help, polite words, and mutual respect were exchanged. Where is this now?

Most people look at the world like a machine — a competition for who is the best and most effective. And then wonder why they are so easily replaceable by artificial intelligence.

DISCERNMENT: HOW DO YOUR EMOTIONS AFFECT MORAL DECISION-MAKING?

Most people should instead question their beliefs before challenging mine. Because I am not the only one speaking the truth. There are many on the planet. Once you focus on the truth rather than in knowing who they are, you will find them all.

I spent my entire life being rejected for speaking the truth. I was expelled from school many times, was insulted by college professors for seeing more than others and asking questions nobody dared to ask, faced bullying and discrimination both in society and in the family, and lost many jobs because of envy and resentment related to what I say. I am not going to change now and make all the morons of the world feel like they won anything. That is not why I became an author. I would rather die free than live as a slave to the world.

There are those who interpret the speakers of the truth as Indigo but what makes me special is the specific contact I mention in my books, and that few have.

Having such contact, however, doesn't mean I am more easily accepted by the masses.

Chapter 26 - How Leaders Manipulate the Masses

Many people asked me about lives on other planets, and I told them what I know, but they didn't believe anything I say. Most live in a fantasy world. They want the truth to fit their expectations. And there is nothing I can do about it, even though I do believe that there are many more people like me in this period of time, as there have always been in other periods.

Most, like me, wrote books. Others, like Tesla, have created technological advances. And others, like Christ, founded their own religion.

Then human beings corrupted religions and created ideological fantasies and schizophrenic group hallucinations, like today's Christianity, hid Tesla's inventions, to keep humanity enslaved to oil, gas, and other quantifiable terrestrial resources, and the many books of tremendous value were burned. Those who read such books were burned too, and everything was lost in time.

You cannot gain awareness and ignore these facts about human nature.

The human being is very primitive and imbecile. That's why people like me come here. In general, more to suffer than to create something.

There is not enough mental mass on earth to create. We can only fertilize this general mass with the truth.

Not everyone is prepared to receive it. Most people want to judge their reality with feelings, but feelings are not conclusive.

If you approach me, for example, and your heart starts beating too fast, with the blood flowing rapidly in your veins, and your mental capacity changes, you will feel that you are in danger. If what I say changes your personal beliefs, you will think that I manipulated you. You will feel cognitive dissonance, which is very unpleasant.

If in spite of all this, you become different and don't recognize yourself in the new person, you will think that I am a demon who has completely changed you.

These are all feelings, and all of these conclusions would be wrong. However, these are experiences that many people claim feeling in my presence.

If your vibration is low, you will find that my vibration is low and that someone else's low vibration is really high. This is also a conclusion that many may make based on their feelings.

From what I have observed around the world, conclusions based on feelings are a common behavior, predominantly in the female gender, and almost always lead to conflicts and misunderstandings.

I remember that a feminist once asked me:

— "Why do you hate feminists?"

— "Did I say that?", I replied to her.

— "No, but that's what I feel", she answered.

— "A feeling, doesn't make a truth", I resumed.

She was confused because most people are comfortable with their feelings. They disregard the truth. They can't analyze the truth except through what they feel.

The problem with feelings is that they can easily be manipulated.

Many men can understand this, even though more and more men seem to have a female perspective of reality too, based on their feelings.

On the other hand, I have noticed that most women can't understand it. They insist that their feelings represent the truth.

When we talk about "female power" and when the world keeps giving more power to women, this is exactly what the world is doing: Empowering feelings over reason.

We see this everywhere these days. People have strong beliefs because they feel it, even though they don't know the truth, and insist on rationalizing their own emotions to justify their words.

Another problem that is common with people who allow themselves to be guided by feelings, is that, because they ignore their own reasoning, they assume that what others speak is based on opinions. They have to deny the reasoning of others, in order to ignore their own.

How much logic do you think is possible in such a society? That is another step downwards, towards ignorance. Because one thing is not to know, and another thing, worse, is not wanting to know. But even worse than that, is when you think your emotions are the source of your knowledge. That's as absurd as one can get.

"I didn't read the book but I can feel what is inside". Does this make any sense? That's exactly what the masses are doing these days.

What value do they then have when compared to a robot? And why should anyone employ a person that rationalizes with feelings?

It is a great logic to follow when you want to lose your freedom. And yet, large masses of people follow speakers, authors, and gurus that base their speech on feelings.

When combined with politics, spirituality, and pharmaceutical lobbies, feelings become the most profitable asset in the world. You can manipulate feelings and then harvest them through antidepressants and vaccination to control a whole society.

Aldous Huxley warned us about such a society. He said, "There will be a pharmacological method of making people love their servitude, and producing dictatorship without tears, so to speak, producing a kind of painless concentration camp for entire societies, so that people will in fact have their liberties taken away from them, but will rather enjoy it because they will be distracted from any desire to rebel by propaganda or brainwashing, or brainwashing enhanced by pharmacological methods. And this seems to be the final revolution".

Chapter 27 - The Truth Isn't Relative to Emotions

Much of the work I had to do with my life came from the world behind the veil, more than from the people I got to know because they really don't know anything. Therefore, I don't care about what people feel, assume or want, when I'm analyzing the truth and exposing it.

That doesn't mean I am not interested in the people who read my books. Many readers have tried, and continue to try, to contact me, and I have allowed myself to be more exposed to also know them, and know what they are looking for, and why they trust me more than other writers.

This attitude helps me know myself through them, and in doing so, also write better. It improves my capacity to do better and helps the readers in their path for the truth.

I believe that it is impossible for there to be a balance without the participation of both parties. And this happens in business and art, as much as in relationships.

In general, people participate fully on a sexual level, but they then forget everything else and become abusive like spoiled children. When their relationships fail, they feel victimized and gain amnesia in regard to the true occurrences in the past. Their brain fabricates a new past, that best aligns with their personal interests. And, in doing so, they perpetuate their past into the future.

It takes a long time for the current and common human to realize that he is the cause of his own karma. But one needs an almost supernatural ability to deal with such people and patience that surpasses self-esteem.

I say this, because most people lie a lot, manipulate, and then complain that no one values them.

Some of the women who lied a lot to me, cried because I didn't believe them anymore. People want others to believe when they lie and also when they tell the truth. Then they complain that others also lie to them. Indeed, they tend to feel more comfortable with those who don't call them on their lies, because many of such people are lying to, just better. And that's how liars betray themselves.

The more someone lies, the less she is able to know whom to trust. She ends up betraying those who trust her and being betrayed by those she trusts.

I believe that many of these women preferred to be cheated by me as this way they would have an excuse to give to friends and family. It is harder when I reject a person for no other reason than their personality. Most women can't handle this type of rejection, which is actually the one they need the most.

I see women repeating too much that men cheat, when in fact they cheat a lot more and more easily than men do.

The reason why women like the "men cheat" argument, is because it distracts the listeners from their lack of responsibility in the three stages of the relationship:

- Stage one — The men they choose and why, with which criteria, being often mostly based on lust rather than love;

- Stage two — The behaviors and words they use in their relationships, greatly motivated by selfishness;

- Stage three — How they punish their men for what they do, in order to force them to destroy the relationship they don't want anymore.

Most people create their fate but few will ever admit it.

The vast majority of these people don't learn, don't change, and they then make others lose years of their life in endless cycles of drama that end nowhere.

DISCERNMENT: HOW DO YOUR EMOTIONS AFFECT MORAL DECISION-MAKING?

I've been in relationships that, three and five years later, ended exactly as I knew they were going to end after a month with such women. I simply gave them opportunities to change. But as I said before, they cannot. Instead, they insisted they wanted to get married because they think that was how their problem would be solved.

They never considered such marriage would most likely end in divorce.

If I was as dumb as many people are, I would have been married about ten times already.

The reasons why people act like this are many. Although there is a lot of ignorance, and there are also karmic reasons, that is, stupidity that goes beyond the current relationships, previous relationships, and into past lives.

When I try to force the solution, karma comes in more strongly. But such people cannot see this because they have a limited view of life. Only after many illusory relationships end and they go through years of suffering, do they understand the mistakes they have made. But then it is too late.

Chapter 28 - Why Many Women Are Single and Lonely

A female friend told me recently that she was afraid to end up single in life.

I tried to explain to her why women end up single and alone but she could not understand. I said to her the following:

— "If you want a man that can't cheat, you must choose a man that no other woman wants. This man should be very ugly, poor, and ignorant. Otherwise, you are in competition with other women. If you are in such a competition, being beautiful isn't enough, because the world is full of beautiful women, and men of value know this, as they can have access to many of such women and meet them regularly. In order to compete with other women, you need more than beauty, because beauty fades away after thirty, and especially after forty. You need to know how to cook, clean, but above all, be very polite, respectful, and friendly. If you are always complaining and insulting, you have very little to offer. And if you want to be a horrible human being with only physical beauty, you will attract men that see exactly only that, and want only that, because, in fact, that's really all you can offer. If you don't want to improve your personality and develop skills that are needed in a relationship, then your only option is to find cats and live with them instead."

After I said these things, she became very angry, blocked my contact, and vanished.

This is the typical behavior of women who refuse the truth. They insist on trying to build a life based on fantasies and then develop victimhood — the idea that they are not responsible for anything in their life.

This is very problematic, especially, if society, as a whole, keeps telling women the same things.

Blaming others for women's problems is actually stealing from them their own independence as a woman. And how independent is a woman who can't be responsible for anything? As independent as a toddler!

When a man has to be the only one responsible for the bills, the cooking, the cleaning, and the planning of the travels, the family budget, and even the social life, he is not acting like a husband or boyfriend but a babysitter.

If in my relationships, I had to do all these things, because the women did not want to do anything, and felt oppressed and bored, then I was nothing more than their babysitter. But for how long do you think babysitting an adult with a sense of entitlement and a lack of character but a very bad attitude lasts?

Even the most patient of men are doing a big disservice to themselves and society when accepting such women.

In other words, that friend that disappeared after receiving the truth is exactly where she should be in life.

It is worse when such women become single mothers because they then perpetuate the same characteristics of entitlement, laziness, selfishness, and lack of character into the next generations.

The more single mothers we have in this world, the more we will see such traits in both men and women.

It then comes a point in time, in which education can't do anything to change the situation, and the only solution to eliminate this plague of criminals and unemployed people with no skills or will to work, is a friendly extermination of the masses, as what we are witnessing now through the use of bioweapons.

Quite frankly, society can't survive with a majority of selfish and lazy people, and not just relationships. A relationship is the basis of society, and if marriages fail, society fails too, and for the same reasons.

Chapter 29 - How an Ascension Occurs on Earth

The reason why so many questions related to love, morals, and commitment seem difficult to answer, is because the vast majority of the sciences of the mind are still in a very primitive state.

You can't really expect much from psychology, neurology, or psychiatry when the ones doing this researchers are not prepared to face a new world, completely different from the one in which they have lived.

That doesn't mean the planet has no hope. This hope comes in the form of the Indigo and other souls coming from different parts of the galaxy to uplift the planet with new insights and observations.

There are many Indigo on the planet, but from what I have analyzed, psychology is far behind from understanding these type of human beings. Psychology is more a religion of divination than a science.

Many of those who are identified as Indigo, are souls with high creative quality, who lived on Earth before.

There is no linear evolution, as we were taught, but rather cyclical, with highly evolved souls living in different historical periods. And the same is true of the Indigo, who did not start appearing in the 1980s as it is said. On the contrary, they have always existed.

Many come and go several times. That is to say, they reincarnate on Earth and on other planets, in different periods.

The concept of time itself is relative, therefore there is no evolutionary linearity even among the Indigo.

When a terrestrial soul gains a sufficient level of consciousness to be able to be reborn on another existential plane, this also happens. And, in a way, all Earthly souls can be considered indigo, because they come from other planets.

When we speak of Earthly souls, we are in essence referring to people who have been reborn on earth for thousands of years and have very heavy karma.

That is why it is said that terrestrials live in a psychiatric hospital or an interplanetary prison. Earth is for sick or very low-vibrating souls.

There is no better description of hell than the Earth itself for an Indigo. Because the Indigo, in this case, to which I refer, is a soul that has vivid and recent memories of previous existences, in more evolved planes of life. And this makes their own life on earth much more difficult and painful.

The indigo feels separated from his natural environment and does not feel that he can understand terrestrial behaviors and thoughts. In general, they have difficulties in socializing and in studying and learning.

The whole existence of these is a catastrophe. Many times they are perceived as crazy and medicated.

Very few indigos are even recognized by society. Most pass through here without being recognized.

Nonetheless, the change they create is factual. This change comes about through their thought patterns.

In general, I do not judge others, but it is easy for me to see who is or not an Indigo by their actions and thoughts.

A lot of people who identify me as Indigo, and say they are too, usually are not. But they think that identifying themselves as Indigo makes them special, and if I say they're not, the whole fantasy falls apart.

There is nothing special about being or not being indigo. Let's say that, whoever you are, has a lot to offer the world. Being Indigo is not a social catalog, but a reference.

Many do not understand this because this planet lives very much centered on appearance.

DISCERNMENT: HOW DO YOUR EMOTIONS AFFECT MORAL DECISION-MAKING?

If I wear an old coat, I am treated one way, and if I wear an expensive coat, I am treated differently, and people even want to sit at the same table and have a conversation with me.

This, in spirituality, is called social blindness. That is why it is said in secret societies that this is a world of blind people or the undead. The people here are not yet awake.

Chapter 30 - Why You Should't Fear Being Different

Some people are quite different from others, due to the experiences they have had in past lives. These experiences can have many causes. They may have been queens and kings, high priestesses or priests, or members of society who possessed much more knowledge even for today's understanding.

Pythagoreans, for example, were more advanced than modern Freemasons and Rosicrucians.

There are also souls who were closer to certain historical personalities, and for this reason reveal a different tendency from the majority.

Still going back to the Indigo case, there are many people who are not, but are in contact with extraterrestrial civilizations. This is not occurring as a physical contact but psychological.

People of good morals tend to attract this contact. And if they are Christian or from another religious faith, they may assume they are communicating with angels or God.

The problem begins when they then try to match what they receive with their own religion or the type of life we have on Earth.

There are many people who ask me about lives on other planets and then say that I have a very fertile imagination or that I am crazy in the head because they don't want to accept what I say.

Most people on this planet are very ignorant, and instead of taking the opportunities to learn, they insult. That is why certain information is not revealed.

I have been identified as indigo by many people all my life, but I never gave it any importance. I read about it but it all seemed too esoteric, and I have always been practical in my life.

For me, the concept of an interplanetary family is very real, but also very practical. There is nothing mystical about it. I have applied everything I learned from other civilizations in my life, to improve it and improve myself, and I have also used to help others, with their physical health, mental health, and learning.

Almost everything I know is already exposed in my books. In fact, the more I wrote, the more my awareness of my past lives on other planets increased.

I had many dreams about lives on other planets since I was a child, but I never gave it any importance. I could not understand what I was seeing anyway. It was when I started writing that my brain changed, and everything that was in the unconscious came to consciousness. Then I started to have a living awareness of everything I knew before.

As I am practical, and above all, an investigator, I continued to doubt my views. But I applied a lot of that knowledge to help children with learning disabilities, teenagers, and even adults, and it worked. Not only did I turn these individuals into real geniuses, with top marks in everything, but helped them get into college.

Unfortunately, even though I wrote about that in a book that could revolutionize the planet, most people are not interested in changing the educational system or the way they learn. Much of what I said on this topic is forgotten and ignored.

Later in life, I took courses in therapy and past life regression, and through the exercises, I was able to understand, more than who I was, how I can identify what is or is not a past life. What this knowledge showed me, was something different and unexpected.

Many people of religions who talk about past lives, do not really believe in the subject, and many people who believe in past lives, have no idea what they say when referring to the topic.

Another change in me that emerged from this experience, was the need to visit museums. Something I do often now. Because it helps me in understanding the current state of people.

DISCERNMENT: HOW DO YOUR EMOTIONS AFFECT MORAL DECISION-MAKING?

Just visiting a medieval torture museum allows recognizing the number of people who have been subjected to horrendous torture, and know why most avoid reading and knowledge in general. They have a subconscious fear of evolving because the fear of torture and death is still present in them.

That is why they ridicule writers, or something more than the reality where they live. The stupidity of these people arises from a tremendous fear of dying, which no longer makes sense, but is still present in their spirit.

In addition, I started to understand better, how the majority manifest tendencies of previous lives and who they could have been.

I also understood better my previous lives on earth. As I understand it, I am a traveler not only from here but from the whole galaxy. So, let's say that I have become more at peace with my constant anxiety regarding meeting new people.

China helped me a lot in this evolution, just because it looks like another planet when compared to Europe.

That was the first impression I had when I got there. From then on, and with the many experiences I had, when traveling through different cultures, my mind was opening up even more to the possibilities, and memories of past lives came more often.

There is a correlation between experience and knowledge, understanding, and the unveiling of our subconscious mind. The more we see and comprehend, the more we know ourselves, and in that knowing, everything about our past comes to the surface.

Not only do you get more memories of your childhood traumas and other past memories, when opening space in the universe outside your body and inside it, but also get access to memories from other existences.

Chapter 31 - Discovering and Accepting the Unknown

I believe most people are not ready for what I say about other planets, because they expect it to match their understanding and beliefs of what life should be.

When I reveal to them something higher than their own understanding, they react with distrust and apprehension, because they are not ready to accept it. Most of what occurs on other planets has no similarity to Earth. In many cases, yes, but in many other cases no.

In other words, science fiction films are manifestations of the terrestrial imagination and do not correspond to what is happening on other planets.

I think people are waiting for me to say something similar to what they watch on television, or that what I say be explained by the films we all see, and are shocked when it doesn't.

On the other hand, there are also a lot of people on this planet lying. And many who come to me are waiting for me to say something that corresponds to the lies they have heard. And are then surprised when that doesn't happen.

Sometimes I like to analyze what is known about the subject on this planet, and I like to listen to people who talk about the topic. And it is easy for me to see who is lying or not from the descriptions they make.

In this sense, I can tell you that the vast majority of spiritual gurus lie. Many movies with people who claim to channel extraterrestrials do not correspond to the truth. These people are either mentally ill or possessed, despite having in several cases quite many followers.

The former soldiers and employees of the American government, who have been speaking publicly recently, may not even have followers, many may not even be heard of them before, but what they have said corresponds exactly to what I know.

I think most people in the spiritual field don't like to listen to those former militaries, because they tend to have a libertine view on life, and don't want to know that other planets tend to be much more organized and controlled than Earth is.

They also expect to hear something related to orgies and free love, and can't believe extraterrestrials have families too and believe in conditional love.

From my personal experience, these two tend to be the topics that those who are curious about alien life reject most.

The vast majority is not ready to be confronted with the possibility of life on other planets, because it contradicts the reality in which they want to believe. It will drive them insane. And that's why they rather call me crazy instead.

For most people, even understanding their own life on this planet, is a great challenge.

I believe that many go back to where they were before, by traveling or reincarnation, to either understand or correct something, and we tend to meet the same people.

It is intriguing, for example, that, when I was in Spain, I had friends from Malta, the United States, South America, but very few Spanish friends. The few Spanish friends I had, were all associated with secret societies, such as the Freemasons and Rosicrucians.

There was only one Christian who didn't seem to fit the rest, until he showed me all the books he had on Egyptian mythology, and told me that he reads everything. In other words, a false Christian, or a pseudo-Christian, because he was afraid to distance himself from the Bible, but was always asking me questions about secret societies and what they study, asking me for books to read, etc.

It is very likely that I had been a Templar during medieval times in Spain. It is possible as well that this Christian was one of the people to be tortured and killed at the stake. People tend to repeat their traumas, in this life and in the lives to follow.

DISCERNMENT: HOW DO YOUR EMOTIONS AFFECT MORAL DECISION-MAKING?

Deep down, people like me come into their lives, not to learn, but to teach them.

They cannot see it, so they do not take the opportunity that life offers them to correct the past and evolve.

I believe that there is a reason why we reincarnate in certain countries, but we are not born to suffer. If a nation does not value us, we have the right to continue our spiritual path in other parts of the world.

In fact, I don't like the idea of nation, and I think it's ridiculous for people to be proud of the country they were born in.

Most people are too attached to their genetics and appearance but how culture affects us is much more important.

China, for example, had a strong impact on me. I always had many Chinese friends, we understood each other well, although we spoke in English. And many said that I was the only foreigner they knew who understood their way of thinking.

I did not absorb the language, but I did absorb the thought structure of the culture.

Also, in terms of food, I changed radically, and today I have a more Asian diet, although I cannot deny what I know about other planets.

In other words, I also apply what I have learned from other civilizations, but I must not be the only one, because it is based on using liquids as ways to balance the spiritual body and heal it, i.e., mostly, using fruit juices.

Chapter 32 - How Cultures Determine Individual Thoughts

Some cultures had a positive impact on me and others had a very negative one, but I can only learn from those that have something to offer. When a culture is degrading and has nothing to give, I learn nothing. So I only have bad things to say about Lithuania and Poland.

I believe that Spain has had a positive impact on me, despite not liking much in that country, and Italy too. I have always made short trips, of weeks only, to Italy, but it is a country that always has a strong impact on my mind.

In relation to people, I feel like an Italian in the midst of Italians, and like a Spanish in the midst of Spaniards. With South Americans, we can talk for hours and hours, and, in the end, we don't remember anything. But with Portuguese, Lithuanians, and Poles, I really feel like an extraterrestrial in their midst. I say one thing and they answer another. In Portugal, they even answer me in English when I speak in Portuguese.

They are people that irritate me deeply. The Portuguese are very ignorant, melancholic, selfish, and envious. Conversations always start and end in the same place. They are unable to see the most obvious. But Lithuanians can be worse, because Lithuanians imagine things that don't exist, just so they can insult someone, often based on xenophobic and racist assumptions.

Some would say you can't discriminate a whole nation based on the behaviors of a majority, and I agree with them, but only to the extent that this affirmation nullifies itself when you use the characteristics of culture to identify a group of people, or you give them passports, and they are then forced to represent what the majority of the people of their country are doing throughout the world. Besides, I don't buy a bag full of rotten apples because one is still looking good.

I have friends from all the countries where I have been, but if that's one or two out of two thousand, or two out of twenty years in that country, the ratio doesn't seem favorable in my eyes.

I can also say that sometimes Lithuanians don't insult on purpose. They insult because they are inside the patterns of a culture that promotes stupid behaviors and even encourages them.

I remember a Lithuanian medical student who was walking with me once and said:

— "If you are not a writer, but you make money selling drugs, you can tell me, and I am still your friend."

Well, I appreciate the gesture of friendship, but the stupidity of the statement was more than I could tolerate and I never spoke to her again.

I have many similar records in my memory of that country, like when they accused me at the cafeteria of stealing a cake, because when I went to get the coffee, I said I had paid for the cake too, and they answered I had taken it already and was trying to get another one for free. Or the moment when five security guards came to me and surrounded my table, speaking in Russian, because they thought I was a spy. When asked for the reasons, they replied:

— "You have been drinking coffee and reading a book for three hours, and we think this is very strange".

Yes, it is very strange that a man like me reads for three hours at the table of a coffee shop in a shopping mall. Therefore I must be a Russian spy.

Lithuanian people are so stupid that it is hard to believe. They really thought I was a Russian spy drinking coffee at a mall.

I've seen so much insanity, stupidity, racism, xenophobia, and schizophrenic attitudes on this planet, that I have decided to spend most of my time in countries where I am left alone and at peace.

That's why I like Croatia. Nobody asks me anything and nobody wants to know what I do or don't do. Nobody looks at me on the street, and I can have a normal life.

DISCERNMENT: HOW DO YOUR EMOTIONS AFFECT MORAL DECISION-MAKING?

I don't know for how long I will live in Croatia, but for now this is a country I can recommend to those who want to feel normal in this world of freaks.

The fact that nobody suspects I am a writer and doesn't even believe when I say it, makes it easier for you, the reader, to know the truth. The thousands of people that cross my path have no idea I will always be writing about them.

If they believed I was a writer, or knew it, they would probably pretend to be friendlier than they are. Like the Portuguese and the Spanish, when they meet someone of white skin and blond, and immediately assume such person must be rich and willing to spend his or her money on them.

I remember once I was walking with a Lithuanian girlfriend in Portugal and they started talking to her and invited her for a meeting to show her property in the region.

What a joke! She was a poor accountant. I had a lot more money than she did. But when people are very stupid and racist, they assume the darker the skin, the poorer one must be.

That's why I believe some cultures and countries should be eliminated from the map of the world. The faster the racists are led to extinction to join the dinosaurs, the faster this planet can heal and evolve.

Chapter 33 - The Alignment of Faith with Life

When a person tries to understand me by connecting events of my past, nothing makes sense, because I did not receive anything from my family or country of birth. I was humiliated, insulted, and disrespected during most of my existence. I was also expelled from school many times for disrespecting the teachers, and had difficulties learning.

I then changed by reading many books, helping myself, and joining many religious groups.

There is no connection between my family or my country and me. Who I am, I built it alone.

In a way, my true family was found in all the religions where I have been because they helped me overcome many problems and taught me the values that I needed.

No religion is perfect but I learned enough from them to improve myself and improve my life.

It was also in these religions that I understood who I am and was able to free myself from the psychological hell where I lived.

I studied many religions and through the many books I was reading, for the first time I was learning about my true self. And that person that I found in me was very different from the one I was told to believe. That's when I really changed. But I didn't become strange to my true self. I became who I was born to be.

It's almost like I was born among demons who didn't want me to wake up. Everything that I found about myself and that helped me progress, was given to me by the invisible world, including my first trips. I had no money to travel when I received a job offer from abroad. And nobody wanted to lend me anything either. But the bank called me to offer me the money, although I did not even ask the bank for that money.

If I depended on my family and friends for anything, I'd probably already be dead. That is why I always tried to keep close contact with everyone in the religious groups where I had been.

Unfortunately, that was not possible for different reasons, but mainly due to a lack of exclusivity.

People always expect me to have only one religion and feel very insulted if I learn from many.

I do not represent any religion and it is impossible for me to be exclusive to one religion only.

Many, very stupid, call this cherry-picking. It is cherry-picking for the stupid. For me, it is getting the truth from a wider and more complete approach to reality.

I would not know who I am if I was being dogmatic. I had to research as much as I could find, in any way that was available.

Today, my beliefs can be labeled dogmatic, because I do have strong beliefs on many topics that will never change. But those beliefs are related to the truth. Not a truth in which I choose to believe, but a truth I know for a fact to be true.

My ability to write books came very late because, as you can imagine, my life was going in the opposite direction.

I do have good memories of my past, but my good memories were created by myself.

Before I even finished college, I was already working as an expert in learning disabilities, and in that work, I helped many children who were hopeless and could not learn by themselves. Many of them had psychologists but they still had poor results in school.

I transformed them into geniuses, capable of learning and remembering anything. And those are the only good memories I have of the past.

I have helped many people even before writing books.

DISCERNMENT: HOW DO YOUR EMOTIONS AFFECT MORAL DECISION-MAKING?

This is another thing that people cannot imagine about my past. They believe that one day I woke up and decided to write. Not at all! All my books come from experiences.

Later, however, I began to receive more information, beyond what I knew about my past lives. And that's when it became impossible to answer the question that everyone keeps asking me:

— "How do you have so much knowledge?"

I cannot answer this, because my knowledge comes from many different areas. It is no longer just knowledge. It's the truth. I received this truth in my mind, in my dreams, in the religions where I was, and I confirmed it by helping really many people.

It is as if the truth was already within me, and I was pushed to accept it and reveal it to the world.

When readers now tell me they find my books after asking God for answers, I get another confirmation, and despite much of my knowledge at the present, I can also receive information when asking God for answers.

Nevertheless, I can't change the world on my own. Having knowledge is not enough. There are many things that are beyond my control.

I also started writing a lot of books on other religions because I realized I could better explain the same topics. But most people can't handle this truth about me. It is very traumatic for them to realize that I am a prophet. The vast majority has to deny this, by asking questions that can confirm to them that I am not such a prophet. They put great efforts to rationalize their beliefs, either towards labeling me insane or some scam artist.

I cannot do anything for them. They are victims of their own stupidity.

In essence, I bring to the world clarity and organization, and in all areas — education, politics, religion, and mental health. This is very obvious in my writings.

The reason why I have so much knowledge in all these areas is also quite obvious. Only a person that has plenty of experience in many alien civilizations can do such things, and evaluate planet Earth effectively.

If people, despite all this information, can't handle the truth, there is really no hope for them. I will leave the planet one day.

Hopefully, there will always be people on Earth that can get this knowledge and apply it to help Earth evolve. And so, in a way, it is better to write books than to speak, because whatsoever I speak, would most likely be forgotten. And yet, I do prefer to speak to crowds than to write alone.

Meanwhile, the impact I am having in the world, already seems to cover many areas, because I wrote under different pen names and I am seeing this world changing according to what I said, namely, in what concerns politics. I got a message from Pakistan recently, thanking me for what I explained about Communism because he said it can save their nation.

Chapter 34 - The Correlation Between Power and Influence

It is complicated when we say, "You know, my true personality, is to always be happy, praising others, and making new friends". We usually assume to be a type of person that may not be what others see in us.

If people look at me, they will probably not see anything that matches what I believe about myself, for example.

We are always affected by our environment. Basically, the environment and our work will condition our personality. Therefore, there is nothing wrong with getting angry, when we feel outside the ideal balance.

What is truly worrying for me are the ones who learn to be happy in the midst of insane people or want to maintain friendships with envious individuals, as there's no reason to accept that which makes us feel miserable. In fact, the more you evolve, the more likely you are to feel miserable in most environments.

Those who tell me they want to change the world or help mankind are being delusional with themselves if not aware of these truths. Because what you can do is influence, plant seeds, and touch those who are prepared for that change.

It also depends on what you intend to do. Not all changes are good. Quite a lot of the evilest people in this world had very good intentions. Besides, when the wrong people read my books, for example, they can create negative outcomes with the same knowledge that is meant to help the majority.

That is why my books follow certain specific patterns in the way they are written. I do it on purpose to make it difficult to use the same knowledge for evil.

I don't even think that people filled with egotistic desires are interested in what I write. They can't find what they seek because it is veiled from them with the strategies I use. Only those who are pure in their intentions can find the truth behind my words.

When you allow yourself to be influenced by culture, rather than the truth, your existence heads in a very different direction.

Lithuania and Poland are examples of what happens to a nation when the vibration is so low that it influences people's culture and behavior and even their ability to observe. To those who have to explore their spirituality in these countries, the truth is a very big mystery, until they leave the territory and it then, suddenly, becomes obvious.

It is only natural that the most spiritual love to travel because that's how you change enough to break free from the ties that culture has on you, and are then able to embrace higher truths, with a new mind and a new capacity to become a new self, developing a new personality.

As your personality becomes more fluid, due to the many influences in your astral body, you also become more aware of your true self.

That won't make you more peaceful but more restless. Peace comes only when you find an environment where you can express yourself fully.

Many of the most spiritual Chinese I met in my life, found that opportunity only in Thailand and Taiwan, and for obvious reasons. You can't be spiritual in a nation oppressed by Communism.

Being a friendly and welcoming person isn't always enough. Quite often it will lead you to disappointment, betrayal, and insults.

Most people are not even prepared to accept kindness.

The Chinese Communists were afraid of me because they realized that I was very popular with students and the students liked me, and even dramatically changed their way of thinking because of my classes. They analyzed on surveillance cameras what I did and said it was impossible to know how I did it. Some asked me:

— "Do you manipulate students?"

— "My job is to teach; If everything is recorded and you cannot see anything strange, it is because there is nothing to see", I said to them.

This does not mean that there were no problems. They entered my apartment all the time, spied on my computer, and sent people to investigate me wherever I went in the city.

I was once poisoned too. That's why I left that country. But all I did was make my students brighter and more capable of thinking for themselves.

The fact that I was loved by many was the reason why I was such a threat.

Social influence is both a thing everyone wants and everyone fears. And in most parts of the world, when people claim to want help, they want essentially a type of help that goes in this direction, which means having more money and better psychological skills. They will reject what doesn't align with these perspectives.

Chapter 35 - We Observe According to What We Know

The problems people have to end up conditioning what they seek. They are like rats, conditioned by fear and pain. Everything else passes them by and is ignored, including the skills needed to reach higher levels of understanding about life.

Almost all books are accessible to the public in today's period in history. Anyone can buy them and in most cases get them for free, namely, books with over a hundred years of existence. However, most people don't. They don't care! Therefore, the ignorance of the world is in fact a choice, and no longer a product of class differentiation.

Marxism and Communism are outdated ideologies and serve only the purpose of manipulating the ignorant masses. These ideologies survive today only because the masses are stupid.

Most people choose to ignore the knowledge they need. Most of their decisions are based on fundamental needs, like having friends, belonging somewhere, and getting opportunities to acquire more wealth. That is exactly why they are easily controlled.

This ignorance is evil in itself. Because every time a human being becomes selfish, arrogant, and competitive, he or she falls into the trap of evil. It doesn't matter which religion he or she practices.

So there is actually a lot of evil in this world and I have seen it in all groups. The rest is not as important as the nature of people.

The more scared people are, and the more they fear discrimination, which is the result of mass ignorance, the easier they are to be controlled. And this possibility makes them all evil by default.

The ignorant, the passive, the quiet, the do-gooders, the sheep of the world, are the weapons of evil. Their politeness is nothing but a social mask begging for acceptance.

We may even think that these principles don't apply to religious groups, but these truths are even more present there.

I have been in many groups and read their books, and to my surprise, found that I was reading a lot more than what they do. That made me understand their religion from a different perspective, more truthful than the one they practice.

I also found that most groups are not really following their founders or religious books, but their own ideas. These ideas are rooted in their own beliefs, which when conformed to the beliefs of other members, become the ideology of the group. Then, as if they were all selectively blind, the members claim to follow certain books and ideologies but practice the opposite, or something completely unrelated.

Try showing them that, and you will soon find yourself under attack, targeted for exclusion. This is what always happens, as a result of showing to people their own lies.

I remember when once in an argument with a priest from the catholic church, we came to a point in which he had nothing else to say that could prove me wrong, and that's when he mentioned the words:

— "You either agree or you go find another group."

That was his way of saying, "I have no idea if you are right or wrong, but I choose to believe what I follow, and that makes you wrong for contradicting it."

I have seen this mindset in all religious groups. That's exactly why they are all forms of collective mental illnesses.

Each group has a different name because each represents a different type of mental illness.

DISCERNMENT: HOW DO YOUR EMOTIONS AFFECT MORAL DECISION-MAKING?

You have the schizophrenics, the psychotics, and the narcissists in psychiatry. And in religion, you have other types of mentally sick people called Christians, Buddhists, Indus, Scientologists, etc.

This occurs because of the difficulty that humanity on Earth has in overcoming the dual way of analyzing reality.

Everything must fit into a dichotomy — us and them, right and wrong, true and false, etc.

Chapter 36 - The Deception Caused by Dichotomies

Those who try to overcome the dichotomy in all things of life, fall into another trap — the cognitive dissonance of having to deal with right and wrong simultaneously.

In many cases, they give up and turn to atheism, because they believe it is a shortcut for the truth. And they couldn't be farther from it by doing that.

In the same situation are the ones who decide that all religions are completely wrong, or those who follow a new age ideology, thinking that everything is correct and reality is relative to our own imagination and beliefs.

There are many types of insanity and they all have one thing in common: The trap of dichotomy.

That trap doesn't exist when you consider the middle path or transition between opposites.

When one finds that the people around him are unfriendly, he finds comfort in solitude;

When one finds that the people around him are too stupid, he learns to appreciate the truth;

When one finds that most art is grotesque, he learns to appreciate the forms of the natural world;

When one finds that there is no freedom, he appreciates the one he still has;

When one finds no love, he learns to despise it.

Nothing is right or wrong in the midst of a required balance that promotes survival.

You don't really have any choice when dealing with dichotomies, but learn the lessons they hide behind the veil of separation and isolation.

Most people can't handle these dualities. They allow themselves to be pushed in one direction or another, like sheep, without realizing how those in power, or society as a whole, manipulates them.

If you always feel that you need to choose one side, between one religion or another, feminism and misogyny, fascism and communism, black and white, government and citizens, you and the others, love and no love, you will always be wrong, no matter what your conclusion is, or the rationalization you make of it. And have you noticed that people with strong beliefs have tremendous difficulties in being challenged and change their arguments?

That happens because they have fallen into a very deep pit of dichotomies. In the fear of the force coming from one side, they allow themselves to go deeper into another, not realizing those are two sides of the same illusion.

The one who has some trauma related to this life or another always fights back this trauma by joining some ideology that opposes the creation of future similar traumas. So, in a way, everyone is fighting against himself and not others.

I am not surprised to see that many feminists are more promiscuous than common prostitutes, because the absence of feminism means that they would lose their rights to do whatever they want. They then fight it!

I am also not surprised to see that so many poor people consider the government to be their enemy, and not those who put the government in power, i.e., themselves in their own ignorance, and consider that communism would solve their problems. They are escaping responsibility!

Even artists and writers that cannot find themselves understood by society as a whole, think that the answer to their lack of proper communication abilities is to intellectualize themselves and make their art more grotesque, boring, and ridiculous than already is.

They fight their own integration because that implies being wrong and downgrading their own ego. They want to fight against the elimination of their ego and not the ignorance of society.

Chapter 37 - Darkness and Ignorance

I often say that the difference between being in the dark and finding enlightenment is the difference between being in ignorance and acquiring education.

I want to explain with this that there is no difference between the pentagram associated with evil and a flower of five petals, or between the fairytales of the Bible and the Sumerian texts. But few people can move out of the mental duality and understand what I am saying here. In fact, a satanist that didn't understand the comparison, asked me:

— "How is Satanism "ignorance"?"

I never said Satanism was ignorance. I also never said it represents intelligence. Why does one need answers that go in one way or another?

The dual mindset of the people makes them always associate something in that mental box as either one thing or the other. They can't consider anything beyond the two options in their brain. Therefore, no explanation is sufficient to them.

I tried to tell him that, what I said, applies not only to his but to all religions on earth. The religious form of universal truths that are manifested in nature and the universe makes all religions a form of ignorance. Therefore, It is wiser to study them all and represent none.

After seeing this answer, he requested me to "explain that in simpler terms". And he never got any other answer from me again. Because it is not my job to educate the very stupid.

Once you fall into the trap of considering everything as one or none, me versus them, it takes a huge amount of time, energy, and efforts, to bring you out of that mental hell.

There is no conversation that can be useful enough in that process because it has nothing to do with the questions or answers, but the mental state in which one finds himself. It is, at that point, and fundamentally, a problem of lack of sanity.

The vast majority of the people on this Earth are deeply insane. They have allowed themselves to be tricked and fooled too many times. They are in a mental hell already, like zombies, without any life of their own.

If you could see the world through my eyes, you would literally see walking dead — people walking around without any consciousness of what life is, repeating rituals that they were taught to repeat, in the form of habits, or having conversations that are nothing more than patterns of what could be compared to a game. All their questions and assumptions are predictable.

Once you understand everything I tell you, you will see that the people of this planet are extremely predictable.

Many would say to you, as they tell me, that this would be very bad, to predict everything. Yes, because it is better to be stupid in their mind. They think that by knowing nothing, their life is more interesting. And so, the stupid is not only dumb but also happy to be dumb.

Why do you think more and more people consume drugs, become alcoholics, and get addicted to substances that kill them? Because they worship this habit of making themselves even stupider than they already are.

What hope can you then have about such people, when they keep getting worse as time goes by? You can't have any hope for them.

You can have hope for the next generations. But from what I have noticed, takes many hundreds of years for cultures to break apart and give rise to new ideologies, better than the previous.

More often than not, the new ideologies are a setback when compared to what was created before.

DISCERNMENT: HOW DO YOUR EMOTIONS AFFECT MORAL DECISION-MAKING?

Plenty of the best knowledge ever written has been lost or remains ignored, misunderstood, and rejected.

Many of the best explanations, coming from me or other authors that wrote them thousands of years ago, cannot be understood until the person is willing to reach a higher perception of reality. And for that, one needs to necessarily consider both of his contradictory beliefs, in regard to what he accepts and rejects, to be wrong.

That is why I recommend studying everything and accepting nothing.

I have done this, I have been in many religious groups, and accepted none. But I never met another person capable of the same.

I am sure that if I created a religion based on these principles, it would have no one because everyone would fall trap in one of the other already existing religions.

Book Review Request

Dear Reader,

Thank you for purchasing this book!

I would love to know your opinion.

Writing a book review helps in understanding readers and also has an impact on other reader's purchasing decisions. Your opinion matters.

Please write a book review! Your kindness is greatly appreciated!

Books Written By The Author

- 66 Days to Change Your Life: 12 Steps to Effortlessly Remove Mental Blocks, Reprogram Your Brain and Become a Money Magnet

- A New Way of Being: How to Rewire Your Brain and Take Control of Your Life

- Codex Illuminatus: Quotes & Sayings of Dan Desmarques

- Collective Consciousness: How to Transcend Mass Consciousness and Become One With the Universe

- Deception: When Everything You Know about God is Wrong

- Discernment: How Do Your Emotions Affect Moral Decision-Making?

- Find Your Flow: Find Your Flow: How to Get Wisdom and Knowledge from God

- Holistic Psychology: 77 Secrets about the Mind That They Don't Want You to Know

- How to Change the World: The Path of Global Ascension Through Consciousness

- How to Get Lucky: How to Change Your Mind and Get Anything in Life

- How to Study and Understand Anything: Discovering the Secrets of the Greatest Geniuses in History

- Religious Leadership: The 8 Rules Behind Successful Congregations

- Spiritual Warfare: What You Need to Know About Overcoming Adversity

- Technocracy: The New World Order of the Illuminati and The Battle Between Good and Evil

- The 10 Laws of Transmutation: The Multidimensional Power of Your Subconscious Mind

- The 14 Karmic Laws of Love: How to Develop a Healthy and Conscious Relationship With Your Soulmate

- The Antichrist: The Grand Plan of Total Global Enslavement Holistic

- The Awakening: How to Turn Darkness Into Light and Ascend to Higher Dimensions of Existence

- The Evil Within: The Spiritual Battle in Your Mind

- The Hidden Language of God: How to Find a Balance Between Freedom and Responsibility

- The Secret Beliefs of The Illuminati: The Complete Truth About Manifesting Money Using The Law of Attraction That Is Being Hidden From You

- The Secret Empire: The Hidden Truth Behind the Power Elite and the Knights of the New World Order

- The Secret Science of the Soul: How to Transcend Common Sense and Get What You Really Want From Life

- The Spiritual Mechanics of Love: Secrets They Don't Want You to Know about Understanding and Processing Emotions

- Uncommon: Transcending the Lies of the Mental Health Industry

DISCERNMENT: HOW DO YOUR EMOTIONS AFFECT MORAL DECISION-MAKING?

• Your Full Potential: How to Overcome Fear and Solve Any Problem

• Your Soul Purpose: Reincarnation and the Spectrum of Consciousness in Human Evolution

About the Publisher

This book was published by 22 Lions. For more information visit us at www.22Lions.com

www.ingramcontent.com/pod-product-compliance
Lightning Source LLC
Chambersburg PA
CBHW060134100426
42744CB00007B/785